MW01088378

Wholly Citizens

Wholly Citizens

God's Two Realms and Christian Engagement with the World

Joel Biermann

Fortress Press
Minneapolis

WHOLLY CITIZENS

God's Two Realms and Christian Engagement with the World

© Stanely Hauerwas, 1998, "Sanctify Them in the Truth: Holiness Exemplified" and T&T Clark Cornerstones, an imprint of Bloomsbury Publishing Plc.

From Luther's Works 13 © 1956, 1984 Concordia Publishing House. Used with permission. www.cph.org.
From Luther's Works Vol. 26 © 1963, 1991 Concordia Publishing House. Used with permission. www.cph.org.
From Church and State Under God© 1964, 1992 Concordia Publishing House. Used with permission. www.cph.org.

Cover image: American flag at St. Patricks cathedral in New York
© iStock/Thinkstock

Cover design: Tory Herman

Paperback ISBN: 978-1-5064-2035-6

eBook ISBN: 978-1-5064-2225-1

The paper used in this publication meets the minimum requirements of American National Standard for Information Sciences — Permanence of Paper for Printed Library Materials, ANSI Z329.48-1984.

Manufactured in the U.S.A.

This book was produced using Pressbooks.com, and PDF rendering was done by PrinceXML.

for Jeannalee
my sine qua non

*Christianity's greatness does not lie
in its being persuasive to the world,
but in its being hated by the world.*

—Ignatius of Antioch (ca. 108 CE)

Contents

Introduction—Our World and How We See It

We live in a binary age. At least, that is what I have been told. I am no technophile, and have, at best, a studied ambivalence toward the relentless rush of technological innovation and advance, so I am content to trust those who tell me it is so. What I am told is that the modern world is binary at its core. That is to say, it is reliant on the fundamental binary opposition of *off* or *on*, *0* or *1*, both digits captured in what has become the universal symbol identifying any machine's power button. From that simple duality, wondrous things can happen. Were I to offer specific examples of those wonders, they would be outdated and obsolete by the time this text finds its way into print and appears before any reader's eyes—in whatever typical form it may now take as you interact with my words. The familiar paper and ink codex or book that represented the core of knowledge and education through most of my life has stiff digital competition, yielding more and more ground to electronic files and screens. And that is exactly the point: the binary age touches all of our lives in profound and often intimate ways. Not just writing and education, but also entertainment, travel, cooking, communication, art, music, and even worship have all been captured and conformed to the binary age. The connections that link these routine marvels of contemporary life to the fundamental binary opposition that undergirds all digital reality are vastly complicated, of course. But, at the bottom of it all remains the simple choice: 0 or 1, off or on.

While the world in which we now live operates with a binary duality at its core, this polarized distinction appears to be confined almost entirely to the world of technology with limited or nonexistent influence on the thinking of the world's residents. It is axiomatic that people in the West favor an anodyne approach to life, placing a premium on such values as pluralism, toleration, multiculturalism, and the existence of a "gray area" in almost every debate. For most people, the simplicity of binary constructions are far too constricting when it comes to dealing with the complexities of institutions, relationships, worldviews, or human interactions.

Yet, both truths are fully at work in our world. On the one hand, everything is binary and driven by the unyielding digital distinction—off or on, 0 or 1. Yet, on the other hand, nothing is black and white or clear-cut, and sharp distinctions—at first evident—prove on closer inspection and reflection to be merely markers on a continuum of infinite possibilities. Such is the world in which we live.

This book is about two things: the world in which we live and Christian doctrine. The first, we have already discussed; propriety demands, then, a similar introduction of the remaining topic. Much can be said about the doctrine of Christianity. Indeed, I have spent most of my adult life saying things about Christian doctrine—especially from within the particular tradition known as Lutheranism. While any number of avenues might be taken by way of entrance into the vast field that is doctrinal theology, it is fitting for my purposes, and I believe altogether fair and accurate, to consider orthodox Christian doctrine as "a delighting in dualities." And, when it comes to recognizing, preserving, and finally delighting in doctrinal dualities, few do it with as much relish as Lutherans.

Christianity and Duality

There are so many tightly bound pairs that ground and animate a rightly ordered understanding of Christian theology. The foundational distinction between law and gospel reminds us that God's word to his creatures has two sharply different components: the law that curbs, condemns, and directs, and the gospel that liberates, redeems, and enlivens. The paradigm of two kinds of righteousness—one active and carried out by creatures, and the other passive and simply received by creatures—sheds crisp light on what exactly it means to be a human creature. The twofold nature of the baptized human as *simul iustus et peccator*, at once saint and sinner, is readily recognized by every honest believer and points to the conflicted and often complicated reality that defines every Christian. The dual nature of our Lord Jesus, at once completely and fully human and completely and fully divine, obviously occupies an essential place in Christian theology. Another duality—the now and not yet of eschatology—makes clear the certain and present fact of God's salvation in Christ, along with the painful knowledge and experience of salvation that is yet to be fully realized. And then there is the duality that is the particular concern of the work that lies ahead—the distinction between the two realms or kingdoms, a temporal one on the left and a spiritual one on the right. Other pairs easily could be added to this list, but the foregoing is sufficient to make my case. Christian theology, especially when practiced with a Lutheran emphasis, is consummately about dualities. Dualities are deeply embedded in faithful Christian confession. It should be noted that this penchant for dialectical truths that must be held in tension, which is characteristic especially of Lutherans, is not some sectarian peculiarity or willful trait. It is simply the inevitable byproduct of a preoccupation with God's Word incarnate in Christ and revealed in scripture, which is, of course, yet another hallmark of good doctrinal theology. The dualities all spring directly from God's Word.

The observant reader no doubt will recognize a perhaps startling and certainly interesting correlation between what I have declared to be the two foci of this study. At the heart of the contemporary world is a binary reality and at the center of Christian faith, and especially my own Lutheran confession of Christian faith, is a collection of tightly bound dualities. Could this happy correspondence offer a hopeful future for the ascendancy of Lutheran teaching in the modern world? Perhaps a binary-based world will more readily resonate with a theological worldview that, likewise, appreciates the binary core of things and accentuates dualities. Maybe the time is ripe for a sudden surge in the popularity of basic Lutheran sensibilities. But, such hope finds little correspondence in reality. As already noted, the world may be utterly binary in respect to its dependence on technology, but it is decidedly opposed to binary distinctions when it comes to human living and interacting. So, the potential serendipity between world and theology is only a circumstantial correspondence after all, and it is a circumstance that is largely empty and of little practical use—at least in this regard. The arrival of the digital age is not likely to usher in a corresponding surge in the popularity of Lutheran teaching or thinking with its special love of dualisms.

The Problem of Polarities

Still, the reality of dualistic or binary centers pulsing as the heart of both Lutheran confessions of Christian doctrine and the surrounding technological world may yet provide some useful insights as we take up the topic at hand. There is, I believe, a certain inevitability, or at minimum, a certain tendency at work with any duality. Dualities migrate into polarities and paradoxes with a powerful and irresistible force. We all know this from experience. It is so common an outcome as to provoke little notice. Indeed, most people would probably consider the difference between a duality and a polarity trivial enough to count them as synonyms. Thus, the binary either/or becomes the controlling idea, and reality eventually, inevitably reduces to the digital choice between off or on, yes or no, 0 or 1. The tension or duality becomes a binary polarity. *That* this is so seems irrefutable. *Why* this is so could be debated endlessly with little agreement. It may or may not have something to do with the binary core that seems to dominate the reality that we daily encounter. But why dualities reduce to polarities is not actually important. For my purposes, what matters is the fact *that* they do.

The inexorable drive that ends with the complete triumph of the binary core is essential to technology and the resultant marvels that define our world; in fact, the binary choice is a *sine qua non* for most of the work entailed in scientific discovery and inquiry. But, this binary choice of one or the other is devastating to good theology, and it is devastation with an impact that is immediate, pervasive, and all too common. Indeed, the powerful attractive force of the simple binary opposition that seems ultimately to master and control every tension and duality constantly shadows the work of the faithful theologian. Of course, a faithful theologian is anyone who attempts to live in accord with God's will and strives to interpret reality in light of that will. The enticement of the simple and comfortable either/or paradigm sings like the Sirens of old, and threatens the theologian of today with a fate every bit as catastrophic and final as the one that endangered Ulysses and his crew. I am increasingly convinced that the failure to preserve critical tensions in theology without succumbing to a mutually exclusive polarity or binary opposition is the culprit behind almost all errant teaching. Which means that this failure is also largely to blame for any number of problems manifest in insipid, etiolated Christian lives and aimless, atrophied Christian churches.

It may seem that my claim is exaggerated and sensationalized; but I think, if anything, I am being modest in my estimation of the significance of this problem. This is an important idea, which deserves careful explication that will, hopefully, result in understanding. So, in the spirit of clarity and in order to be as lucid and convincing as possible, I will offer some further elaboration. In the realm of theology, there is, I believe, an essential and monumental difference between a duality and binary opposition. Duality describes two aspects of one reality that are distinct and different, but that hang closely together, influence one another, and work together to accomplish some purpose. There is no inherent conflict or incongruity between them. On the contrary, a binary opposition or a polarity describes two things that are held together in stark contrast. They are mutually exclusive—a thing is either one or the other. It is either on or off; it is either black or white. Dualities and polarities are two different things. Of course, it is certainly not lost on me that even to state this truth is to submit to the principle of binary opposition! Which serves as an excellent reminder that I am not arguing that duality is good and polarity is bad. There is a place for each of them. Binary oppositions and polarities typically find their best applications in contexts with empirical metrics such as the hard sciences, or in the construction of a logical argument or the demonstration of some fact. There is ample room for this even in theology.

Still, the two are different, and in the world of theology, duality must not be allowed to degenerate into polarity. Consider, for example, the two natures of Christ. This twofold truth is not a polarity, but a duality. Christ is fully human and fully divine, completely both at once—all the time, for all time. In the hypostatic union in Christ, the two aspects are not mutually exclusive but coexist beautifully and perfectly. Indeed, it is precisely this mutuality and interrelationship of the two distinct natures in one person that is expressed in the traditional but now almost infamous category theologians call the *genus majestaticum*. The human nature is still human nature even as Christ performs divine and fantastic actions, such as walking on water or passing through locked doors. This is Christian truth. But, if the dichotomous reality of Christ's two natures is allowed to slide into a polarity, we are left with an opposition between the human and the divine that can only result in the conquest of one over the other. Jesus ends up being either only human or only divine, or switches back and forth between one or the other as needed—and heterodoxy, and eventually, heresy takes the day. It should be clear that the move from duality to polarity leads away from orthodox Christology and into any one of a host of heretical ideas that have always plagued the church and tempted those bent on finding a reasonable and logical solution—or at least, an explanation—for the mysteries of salvation history. To confess Christ's incarnation faithfully, one must confess the tension implicit in the duality of the two natures fully present and fully active in one person.

Faithful confession must resist the temptation to succumb to the lure of the binary opposition.

Before attending to the business before us, the duality of the two realms of God's activity in this world (more commonly, and inaccurately, known as the "doctrine of the two kingdoms"), one further illustration of the difference between duality and polarity may prove helpful. The distinction between law and gospel is an altogether familiar twofold truth, and it is one that must be seen as a duality and not as a binary polarity. I have made a fuller case for this in other places,[1] but the essence of the argument can be made succinctly. Law and gospel belong together as two components of God's unified and consistent word to his creation. Indeed, God's word is unitary, not schizophrenic, and the distinction between law and gospel is only relevant in the context of a fallen creation. In a broken world, God's law speaks the truth of his will for the right functioning of his world, while God's gospel speaks the word of grace and forgiveness to creatures who always fall helplessly and hopelessly short of that perfect will. This side of Eden, these two words are quite distinct and different, but they are neither mutually exclusive nor even inherently antagonistic. They exist together in a duality.

So, the creature who has heard and (by the gracious working of God's Spirit through the gospel's proclamation) believed the word, lives life in the world now as a new creation and does the things that God created and redeemed her to do. She does God's will. She lives according to the law. This tension or cooperative duality of law and gospel coheres with the standard structure of Paul's letters and Christ's teaching. Allowing the distinction to slip into a polarity, however, leaves us with an antagonistic opposition between the two aspects of God's word in which one—the superior gospel—must ultimately trump the inferior other. In the Western church of recent memory, the outcome has been the painfully familiar antinomianism that inevitably results from law/gospel reductionism. In such a binary atmosphere,

---

1. Joel Biermann, *A Case for Character: Towards a Lutheran Virtue Ethics* (Minneapolis, MN: Fortress Press, 2014), especially pages 115–18.

non-Lutheran Protestants.[4] This is a phenomenon that has generated a fair amount of attention—or more accurately, alarm—in Reformed circles and some cheers and applause in Lutheran camps. I am not among those cheering. From what I have learned, too often, those who are "following Luther's teaching," in fact, are not following his teaching at all. Still, even that problem will likely hold little, if any, interest for most of those who I hope will read this book. No, the problem that most concerns me, and the problem that I will strive to highlight and address, is the fact that even among those who bear his name, Luther's teaching on the two realms is infrequently understood, seldom appreciated, and rarely, if ever, carried out. This is my reason for writing. I am convinced that within much of the Lutheranism that is practiced in North America, the duality of Luther's teaching on the two realms has been obscured, neglected, and largely abandoned. The church and her people and the world around them all suffer mightily for this loss. My objective, then, is to offer Luther's teaching on God's left and right hands of activity to a church that sorely needs to hear and learn again this insightful and fruitful dynamic.

Two Realms and Two Kinds of Righteousness

Before embarking in earnest on this task, however, there remain a few more introduction-appropriate items worthy of discussion, which, if appreciated, may enhance the clarity and perhaps force of my argument. One of these potentially helpful digressions is to consider the interaction between the duality of the two realms and the duality of the two kinds of righteousness, and the way that both of them correlate with the field known as ethics. Ethics—more specifically, and relevantly, *Christian* ethics—is occupied with a Christian's First Article identity and actions—his being and doing in this world. Ethics is not about being right with God, which would be the province of the doctrine of justification, but about being right in all the activities and

---

4. The particulars of this development will be considered more fully in the following chapter, but one example can be found in David VanDrunen, *Living in God's Two Kingdoms: A Biblical Vision for Christianity and Culture* (Wheaton, IL: Crossway, 2010).

responsibilities that define each believer's life.[5] Obviously, one does not earn God's favor or even wrest blessings from God by good behavior or by pious impulses. Justification, as every believer well knows, is the work of God and God alone. One is right before God because of God's work accomplished in Christ's life, death, and resurrection. This should all go without saying, but for clarity's sake, it is being said again.

The gospel-gifts of justification, then, crucial as they are, hold little immediate interest for ethics, but what goes on in the day-to-day realities of life with all of its opportunities, burdens, and responsibilities is a consuming obsession. How one goes about choosing and doing the usually mundane and only occasionally extraordinary sorts of things that define ordinary life is the driving concern of ethics. On cue, the distinction between the two kinds of righteousness makes a well-timed entrance at precisely this point. A Christian is righteous before God in the vertical realm, passively, only by God's work in Christ; and that same believer then pursues a life of righteousness actively before the rest of creation in the horizontal realm. Ethics is limited to the second, horizontal, kind of righteousness—the righteousness of a creature doing what she was created to do. Much more could be said, but this sketch is sufficient for the point that needs to be made: the two kinds of righteousness should not be confused with the distinction between the two realms. They are not the same. All the vital dualities that define and animate Christian theology are not to be understood as mere semantic or doctrinal distinctions lacking any significant real difference and that, in truth, reduce to one foundational, primary, and basic duality , as is sometimes suggested. Each duality is a dynamic and unique tension that describes or summarizes some aspect of God's truth that surrounds and impacts our being. Law and gospel serve to describe the way that God's word strikes fallen creatures in two very different ways. The paradigm of two kinds of righteousness provides a way to think about the existence

---

5. Traditionally, the label *sanctification* is applied to this field of interest. The multiplicity of meanings and ideas associated with this amorphous term, however, severely weaken its continued usefulness for my purposes. But making that case would require an argument that lies outside the current project.

of a creature who lives all of life both before God and before fellow creatures. And the duality of the two realms, or two kingdoms, clarifies the two different ways that God works to accomplish his purposes in this world. Each duality does its own particular work.

Still, there are, of course, strong relations between the dualities, especially between the three now under consideration. God's word of law and gospel speaks the truth of what God expects of his creature as well as the truth of what he has done for that creature—especially what he has done in Christ. The gospel makes the believer righteous before God, and the law tells that same believer how she is to go about living righteously (i.e., in accord with her Creator's will and design) before other creatures. The horizontal righteousness of daily living plays out in the arena of the "left hand" of God's creation and activity. And yet, even as the believer strives in the left hand to live according to God's plan—i.e., God's law—that same believer dwells continually in the right-hand realm of God's grace, and regularly and eagerly receives the comforting and restorative word of the gospel from God's right-hand institution, the church. The mutual interrelation and interdependence of these dualities means that accurate reflection on any one duality hinges on a faithful understanding and account of the others. God's truth is a cohesive, comprehensive, and expansive unity; human creatures, though, are constrained to think about but one thing at a time—at least, the human creature responsible for this book is so constrained. So, in the midst of finely focused discussions about left-hand realities, it is important to bear in mind the wider right-hand facts of faith, and to be assured that I am doing the same.

The Scope of the Temporal Realm

One item that remains before this introduction can at last draw to an end. There is within my tradition a tendency to understand issues pertaining to the right relation of church and state as essentially synonymous with Luther's "teaching of the two kingdoms." That is to say, it is not uncommon for any mention of Luther's teaching on the two realms of God's presence and activity in this world to be received with a comment along the lines of, "Oh, you mean the doctrine of the separation of church and state?" Of course, the right response to that notion is almost always, "No, I don't!" While Luther's teaching on the twofold nature of God's work in this world most definitely speaks directly and relevantly to virtually all questions relating to issues of "church and state," it is not identical to them. There is more, indeed exceedingly more, to Luther's foundational insight into the duality of God's temporal and spiritual fields of activity in this world than merely the distinction between church and state. When Luther distinguishes between the temporal realm of the created world, complete with all who occupy and animate it, and the spiritual realm of God and his eternal verities, he is leaving nothing out. The duality of the temporal and spiritual, or the left and the right hands of God, extends so far and so wide and so deep as to overlook or exclude simply nothing. Certainly, the government and the church both are fully swept up into this comprehensive duality. But so is everything else. Marriage and family, sexuality, education, environment and climate, economics, science, art and music, medicine, diplomacy, friendship, leisure and sports: all of these pursuits and every other pursuit are all encompassed in the distinction between God's two discrete methods of operation within and on behalf of his creation.

Thinking in terms of the creed and its three articles is probably the best way to arrive at an accurate understanding of Luther's two realms. The first article of the creed confesses the work of God the creative Father who makes heaven and earth. This is the purview of the temporal, left-hand realm. If it is part of creation, it is part of the left-hand domain of God's work. The creed's second article, of course, recounts the narrative of salvation history as accomplished by the incarnate Son. The second article gives us the gospel, made necessary, it will be remembered, because of the failure of the creation—or more precisely, the crowning achievement of that creation—to do what it was created to do. The second article is the concern of the right-hand domain of God's work. It answers the question of the creature standing before her Creator. It gives no directives or tasks, but simply gives grace. The right hand makes a sinner right with God. From a human, earthbound standpoint, then, the left/right duality is outrageously out of balance. The left contains everything that makes up every part of every stage of life while the right hand pays attention to only one thing: the delivery of the gospel. Believers, though, understand and treasure the narrow and exclusive focus of the right hand and recognize that from an eternal, "heaven-bound" perspective, the imbalance between left and right is even greater than it first appears . . . but entirely reversed! So, the first article coincides neatly with the concerns of the temporal realm while the second article coheres nicely with the spiritual realm.

While it might seem that aligning a tripartite creed with a duality could only end up with leftovers, even the third article sheds light on the temporal/spiritual pairing. With utmost conviction and confidence, the concluding article points us to the day when through the Spirit's activity, God's purposes are fully and finally realized, the two realms blossom into one unified reality, and the duality is sublated. Like so many of the twofold distinctions within Christian doctrine, the duality of God's left hand and God's right hand applies only during the time between the fall and the eschatological consummation of the creation. On the last day of resurrection and judgment and restoration, God's reign in Christ through the Spirit will be all in all and the distinction between left and right will disappear, along with the distinctions between the law and the gospel and the two kinds of righteousness. At the Parousia, there will be one kingdom of our Lord, one Word from our God, and one righteous identity of each restored creature fully human at last before God and creation. Left and right will no longer be distinguished. But, while we wait now in good hope for that certain last day, the left/right duality remains in full effect, and sheds a great deal of light on the lives that we are to live each day. The world, all of it, is God's and God's people must learn to see every bit of it as God sees it. It is God's good left hand or temporal realm. But, of course, it is broken—broken by our own willful and sinful rebellion against God and his will. And when the brokenness of that first article world smashes and trashes our lives with devastating regularity and unyielding ferocity, as God's called people, we have the right hand, spiritual, reality of Christ's grace to catch us, salve us, and ultimately restore us. Such is the profound truth of the two realms of God's activity.

The Plan of This Book

It should be clear, then, that there is more to the two realms of God's work than issues of church and state. That wide and comprehensive context should be apparent in all that follows—even as I narrow my focus to the specific questions of what it means to be Christian and how we are to be church in relation to a state that is neither Christian nor the church. My plan is uncomplicated. To begin, it seems judicious, and obvious, that a retrieval of good two realms thinking should spend some time listening to the author. I will do that but with a slightly different twist as I take up Luther's teaching in his commentary on Psalm 82. But five centuries lie between the Wittenberg Reformer and the church of today. I will not attempt to cover all of that history, but to gain an understanding of the present situation, it will be helpful briefly to sample and review some of the thinking about the "two kingdoms" that has taken place over the last several decades. With Luther and Lutheran thinking in mind, I will then spell out some specific foundational ideas about the proper distinction and interrelationship of the two realms, looking in particular at the three estates. Once this work is done, all that remains is the all-important application of those ideas to concrete realities: first, to the church as God's right-hand institution in the world and the pastors that serve that church, then to the lives of Christians generally. Finally, I will offer an essay with some thoughts on the inherent challenge that always confronts the church as she and her people strive faithfully to live and deliver the timeless gospel in a broken and ever-changing world—the problem of tradition over against translation.

God's church lives in God's world. Exactly how it goes about doing that is not always as clear or obvious as it might initially seem. And the perpetually variable reality that is our world means that it is impractical and unwise to attempt to remove all ambiguity by addressing every situation or possible scenario that may confront us. Still, if one has the right way of approaching the questions, and can think with clarity about the matters at stake, then it is not necessary to spell out a compete argument for every problem. Simply using the tools of good teaching and lucid insight will enable Christians to consider and draw conclusions about the best way to handle any situation or challenge. The goal of this book is to help form and direct that ongoing process of evaluation and consideration so that it happens in ways that are faithful to scripture and the teaching of the church. When the church's people, parishioners as well as pastors, are so equipped, each of God's two realms will be positioned to accomplish its peculiar purpose, and perhaps, it may even be that the interface between them will grow less murky and perplexing. I do not believe such thinking naïvely optimistic; hopefully, once the argument has been made, the reader will agree.

1

The Legacy of Luther

The year 1530 stands out as particularly significant in the Lutheran narrative. It was on June 25 of that year that Elector John of Saxony, Philip of Hesse, and other faithful princes and rulers of Germany stood before Emperor Charles at Augsburg and presented their confession of faith. It was a political gathering at Augsburg, an imperial diet, and thus it was that politicians and princes read, signed, and received the Confession. Of course, the actual composition of the Augsburg Confession had not been entrusted to statesmen. That task fell to a theologian, with his own political proclivities and capabilities—Philip Melanchthon. Philip hardly acted in isolation; engaged in a lively correspondence with Luther himself, who had been safely deposited in the Koburg castle for the duration of the diet, Philip's confession was ensured as comprehensively Lutheran. The very nature of the Augsburg Confession itself as, at once, highly political and thoroughly theological captures some of the difficulty and dynamism that always swirl around the interface of the state and the church. Of course, the confusion and obfuscation regarding that duality were even greater in the sixteenth century than in the twenty-first—which problem was, of course, precisely one of the precipitating forces behind the Confession and all that preceded it. Fortunately, for my purposes, unpacking the conundrum of medieval church/state chaos and confusion (what Luther deemed a satanic stew) is a problem of history that I can leave to others.

Psalm 82

It was actually a few months before the presentation of the Augsburg Confession that the prolific Luther produced a short commentary on a handful of psalms. Typical of the Wittenberg professor, the reflections were more than mere exegetical explorations and touched on pressing questions of the day. One of those problems received focused attention when Luther took up the eight verses of Psalm 82. The reformer did not miss the opportunity to address the relationship between political powers and rulers and ecclesiastical authority—or more simply, church and state. Luther's commentary on this short psalm serves as a particularly useful source for understanding his teaching of the duality of the two realms. It is useful, I believe, not only because of its brevity, but also because it offers a fresh and more mature presentation of Luther's ideas, coming seven turbulent and busy years after his more familiar and widely cited treatise, "Temporal Authority, to What Extent It Should Be Obeyed." The lecture on Psalm 82 goes far in clarifying his teaching and helps to dispel some of the errant ideas that continue to hound and cling remora-like to Luther's concept of the two realms. The intent of this chapter is to provide a clear and cogent presentation of Luther's teaching on the two realms. This is a task sorely needed, it seems to me, since too often, Luther's ideas are simply criticized or cited as if the actual content of his teaching was universally understood, and so, safely taken for granted.

Luther's Two Realms

In the four quick paragraphs of the preface, Luther lays out the necessary context for his comments. "Once upon a time," he begins, and then relates the sad tale of the old battle between kings and priests—a battle that had, thanks in no small part to his own work, witnessed a decided change in fortunes during Luther's own lifetime.[1] Luther recounts the sorry days when "kings and princes could not ruffle a hair of any monk or priest, no matter how insignificant the maggot was," for fear of the eternal consequences of ecclesiastical excommunication. In typical fashion, Luther bluntly admits that the threat of eternal damnation had proved a marvelously effective restraint on the powers of secular rulers. "The secular rulers were completely subject to these clerical giants and tyrants; and these dissolute, rude fellows walked all over them."[2] But all of this changed with the arrival of Lutheran teaching, more broadly, if less precisely, referred to by Luther as the Gospel: "Now, however, the Gospel has come to light."[3] Of course, as he wrote those words, Luther knew very well that it is the Gospel that brings justification to sinful people, but he also knew that it does more: "It makes a plain distinction between the temporal and the spiritual estate and teaches, besides, that the temporal estate is an ordinance of God which everyone ought to obey and honor."[4] It is but a single sentence of the commentary, but this, certainly, is the crux of the teaching on the two realms, and warrants a bit more explication before resuming Luther's lament about the newly empowered princes.

The teaching was so plain and definitive for Luther that it needed little elaboration—besides, he had already offered such a defense in critical essays written during the previous decade.[5] For Luther, reality splits into two distinct areas, or as he calls them, here, "estates." Luther's terminology for what exactly is distinguished is hardly consistent. He also regularly employs words variously translated as realm, regiment, area of governance, and kingdom, to refer to the two "things" that must be distinguished. The point is the *duality* between

---

1. Jaroslav Pelikan and Helmut T. Lehmann, eds., *Luther's Works*, American Edition, 56 vols. (St. Louis, MO and Philadelphia, PA: Concordia and Fortress Press, 1958–86), vol. 13, 42. "Commentary on Psalm 82."
2. Ibid.
3. Ibid.
4. Ibid.
5. Especially "Temporal Authority" and "Can Soldiers Too Be Saved?," *LW* 45.

what is temporal and what is spiritual. It is also worth noting, or more accurately admitting, that these two terms—temporal and spiritual—seem to be Luther's preferred labels for each of the two realms or estates. What makes this particularly interesting is that a popular contemporary terminology for Luther's duality is to refer to the two hands of God—the left hand for the temporal realm and the right for the spiritual. Yet, the reformer uses these labels only rarely. Neither "hand" puts in an appearance in the lecture on Psalm 82. And the left/right designation also fails to make a showing in either of the two essential essays from the 1520s. In fact, while I know better than to hazard a claim to comprehensiveness in my search, I am aware of only a handful of references to the left/right terminology by the Reformer.[6] So, while many Lutherans, present writer included, find the left/right terminology quite useful, Luther himself seems to have been satisfied with more obvious and less anthropomorphic terminology, such as temporal and spiritual.

A much more significant point arising from Luther's pithy sentence is the final assertion: "the temporal estate is an ordinance of God which everyone ought to obey and honor."[7] This is the essential point from which all else springs. The material world of creation that surrounds us is God's work and still matters to God. It is temporal, indeed, but it is precious to God. Since it matters to God, he provides for its protection and care by establishing what Luther here calls the temporal estate: the rulers and governments who are accountable for the well-being and right functioning of that material, temporal world in which we all live, and in which the spiritual estate carries out its work. The temporal

6. One of the more interesting, called to my attention by my colleague, Paul Raabe, appears in Luther's 1530–1531 lectures on Song of Solomon 2:6, "Let his left hand be under my head, And his right hand embrace me." Luther comments, "Furthermore, he includes here two special blessings belonging to this people: the kingdom, or government, which he calls the left hand, and the priesthood, or worship of God. These embraces, he says, make it possible for this rose to endure the thrust of wild beasts and brambles, since it is wholly within the embrace of God, whether you look at the church or the kingdom, for the Word of God is in both." (*LW* 15, 216). Given the explicit use of the two hands in the verse, Luther's use of the terms here seems almost demanded by the text. Other, less intriguing, instances occur in a 1518 lecture on Psalm 110 (*WA* 1, 692, 3); and two Advent sermons from 1532 (*WA* 36:385, 6) and 1544 (*WA* 52:26, 24). It is worth noting that in all of these cases, there is but one use of the term "left, or left hand." Luther does not make extended use of the verbiage.

7. *LW* 13, 42.

estate is not wicked, tawdry, or suspect. It is not opposed to God or to the spiritual estate. It is not even a necessary evil as a consequence of the brokenness of sin infecting the creation. There is nothing negative or regrettable about the temporal estate. It is simply God's provision for the smooth functioning of the creation. *Temporal-purpose*

All of this becomes exponentially more lucid by considering the first tasks given to the creatures who were the final and crowning work of the world's sixth day. Adam and Eve were placed in the garden to tend it and to rule all its inhabitants. In a very real sense, they were the first to occupy the temporal estate as masters or lords of the creation, responsible for its health and flourishing. Later in his comments on the Psalm, Luther also points to the necessity and significance of seeing this world as the result of God's creative activity, with the communities that govern and tend the creation as the work of God himself: "such communities are God's work, which He daily creates, supports, and increases."[8] Luther is fully convinced of the implicit godliness of these human communities, pointing out that in the Book of Jonah, even Nineveh is called "a city of God."[9] This truth perdures, Luther insists, even when it is ignored or denied by the world's great thinkers: "For mad reason, in its shrewdness, and all the worldly-wise do not know at all that a community is God's creature and His ordinance. They have no other thought about it than that it has come into being by accident."[10] But, the arrangement of the temporal community and the corresponding spiritual community is no accident. The design is God's plan and God's ongoing work. The realms—both the spiritual and the temporal—belong to God and are directed by him for specific and distinct, but equally God-pleasing work.

Although, as admitted, Luther may not have capitalized on the imagery of God's two hands, the metaphor is very apt. It seems to capture exactly Luther's point about the godliness and goodness of the temporal realm. God's two hands work differently, but always in concert, to accomplish God's will. The left is not less God's hand simply

8. Ibid., 47.
9. Ibid., 46.
10. Ibid.

because it has work that is different from that of the right hand. What God gives the temporal rulers to accomplish is important, divinely mandated, and so, holy work. The left hand is not abandoned and consigned to the usurper Satan. It is not the antithesis of the spiritual realm. It is God's left hand, and so, is inherently good. Still, it is obvious to us all that this side of the Fall—the left hand that we know—is shot through with sin, Satanic subterfuge, shame, and pain . . . of course, the same is true of God's right-hand realm the other side of the Fall. Certainly, more can be said about all of this, and in time, some of it will be said; for now, though, it is quite enough to establish the foundational and guiding truth that the temporal estate is God's plan and God's agent. It is the left hand of God.

Augsburg Confession XVI

Before returning to Luther's exposition of the Psalm, this is a convenient juncture for one more brief and worthwhile digression—back once more to the Augsburg Confession, specifically to the text of the Confession's 16th article. In Latin, it is titled simply, "Concerning Civic Affairs"; as usual, the German heading—along with the body of the article itself—is a bit more specific and blunt: "Concerning Public Order and Secular Government."[11] The point of the article is patently and effusively obvious: in the civil realm, "all political authority, orderly government, laws and good order in the world are created and instituted by God."[12]

With a God-pleasing civil realm firmly established, and in direct opposition to the erroneous and dangerous teaching of the Anabaptists, the article is explicit about the sorts of things that could occupy the attention and effort of pious Christian people. "Christians may without sin," the German text asserts, "exercise political authority; be princes and judges; pass sentences and administer justice according to imperial and other existing laws; punish evildoers with

---

11. Robert Kolb and Timothy Wengert, eds., *The Book of Concord* (Minneapolis, MN: Fortress Press, 2000), 48.
12. Ibid.

the sword; wage just wars; serve as soldiers; buy and sell; take required oaths; possess property; be married; etc."[13] Since the civic realm, the temporal world of government and commerce and marriage and family, was God's blessed creation and continued to enjoy his favor and pleasure, not only *could* God's redeemed people participate in the affairs of the mundane and material world, they *should* so participate. Living as a part of the creation, embracing the work, activities, joys, and challenges of life in the flesh and blood world, was seen by Luther and the reformers gathered in Augsburg not as a necessary but reluctant concession to material human existence, but as a holy obligation and happy duty entirely congruent with God's will and purposes.

This exuberant affirmation of the material world complete with all of its supporting structures, activities, and relationships proved to be a transformative and powerful message in Luther's day. It ended the long-established notion of monastic life as a higher path of faithfulness and discipleship, superior to ordinary, workaday, life consumed with the affairs of home, state, and business. If the civic realm was God's good creation and the object of his lavish mercy and grace, then a believer need not fear it nor flee it. "The Gospel does not undermine government or family but completely requires both their preservation as ordinances of God and the exercise of love in these ordinances."[14] This was a radical declaration in 1530, and if rightly appropriated and appreciated, can continue to be every bit as transformative and potent in the early twenty-first century. But, again, more can be said on that later, for now, it is time to bring the digression to a close and return to Luther's work on the psalm.

Pompous Princes

Luther's revolutionary teaching about the civil realm and the divine legitimacy of that realm's temporal powers had an immediate and profound effect on his world—which is at least part of what prompts

13. Ibid.
14. Ibid., 49–51.

his 1530 reflections on Psalm 82. As Luther put it, the tables had been turned: "Now popes, bishops, priests, and monks have to fear and honor the princes and lords and nobles, give them gifts and presents, keep the fasts and the feasts, and worship at their feet as though they were gods."[15] Following a pattern similar to the one established by the peasants only a few years before, the princes had grabbed a nugget of Luther's teaching, twisted it out of context, and turned it to their own purposes.[16] The right balance between the two realms had been lost—destroyed by the overreaching princes and rulers. "They have now discovered a new device," accuses Luther, "and declare that whoever rebukes them is seditious, rebels against the authority ordained by God, and defames their honor. Thus since they are rid of the tyranny of the clergy and cannot be rebuked by them, they now want to be rid of the Gospel and be beyond its rebuke, although it has set them free."[17] The transformation within the lifetime of Luther had been astonishing. The power shift was dramatic and all but complete. The princes had capitalized on the opening afforded by Luther's emphasis on their own divinely appointed and God-pleasing service and exploited the doctrine to cultivate their lust for power. "Their ultimate desire," Luther was sure, "is to be able to do whatever they wish, without hindrance or rebuke, without shame or fear, and with honor and glory."[18] In other words, the princes were only too human.

This, then, was the context for Luther's exploration of Psalm 82. He was witnessing another instance of his own teaching, so confidently and carefully distilled from the Bible, being subverted and cavalierly wielded for self-serving, ungodly ends. In the psalm, Luther found a direct connection with his own situation. "There were such little squires among the Jewish people, too," Luther avers. Rooting the

---

15. *LW* 13, 43.
16. That Luther's teaching and writing was a source of inspiration and encouragement when the peasants revolted against the rulers of the land in the mid 1520s is widely recognized. What is less readily understood is Luther's harsh rebuke of the rebellious peasants. When one rightly grasps the consistency and comprehensiveness of Luther's teaching on the duality of the two realms, however, Luther's shock and dismay at the peasants' revolt is as reasonable as the disdain that he levels at the princes for their abuse of the same doctrine.
17. *LW* 13, 43.
18. Ibid.

presumption of the psalmist's troublesome princes in Exodus 22:8, where Moses calls the leaders "gods," Luther wrote, "They made of this passage a cloak for their shame, and a defense of their iniquity against the preachers and prophets; they would not be rebuked by them, puffed themselves up against their rebukes and their preaching, and struck them on the head with this saying, 'Will you rebuke us and teach us? Do you not know that Moses calls us gods?'"[19] The correlation was exact; for Luther, the words of the Psalm were penned against his own arrogant and self-important princes. Luther's commentary addresses the immediate concern, and highlights the essence of his teaching on the duality of the two realms.

It would have been easy and understandable for Luther to offer an exegetical review of the psalm that delivered a one-sided blast against the overweening princes. But any one-sided route is the death of a duality, and Luther carefully resists the temptation. In fact, he again deliberately establishes the privileged place of God's temporal rulers. "From this we see how high and how glorious God will have rulers held, and that men ought to obey them as His officers and be subject to them with all fear and reverence, as to God Himself."[20] With an eye especially on the memory of the recent chaos known as the Peasants' Revolt, Luther reiterates his disgust with any form of rebellion: "It is not His will to allow the rabble to raise their fist against the rulers or to seize the sword, as if to punish and judge the rulers. No they must leave that alone! It is not God's will, and He has not committed this to them."[21] Immediately, though, Luther checks the egos of the princes, reminding the reader that God himself holds the rulers to account and that the rulers must give heed to God's will as they lead. Both the ruler and the ruled are responsible directly to God to accomplish what each has been given to do in the way that God wills. Thus, another duality (ruler and ruled, or prince and people) is established as a subset within one half of the larger duality of the temporal and spiritual realms. The goal is a smooth-running creation. "On both sides, then, everything will go well,

19. Ibid.
20. Ibid., 44.
21. Ibid.

in the fear of God and in humility. Subjects will have regard for God and gladly be obedient for His sake, and rulers will also have regard for God and do right and keep peace for His sake."[22] God's good creation functioning according to God's good will is the goal, not just Luther's goal, but the inherent goal or telos of the creation itself.

It is important to remember that Luther does not conjure his doctrine according to his own inclinations or agenda. He does not devise or develop his teaching, but merely uncovers and reports what is already there in God's revelation—both the specific revelation of the Word made flesh and the general revelation of the world itself. Luther does not stress the twofold rule of God and the godliness of governing for political or personal reasons. He does it because he is thoroughly convinced that this is the arrangement put in place by God himself. Luther is submissive to the will and Word of God, and so, teaches the twofold rule of God with an appropriate zeal and calculation. The doctrine is true because God has so designed it, and as Luther knew, faithful and accurate teaching is inherently compelling and resonates with the reality of the surrounding created world, and of course, faithful teaching always aligns with what is clearly revealed in the written word of scripture. This was the critical factor animating Luther's alarm and warning leveled at the princes. He saw the princes as culpable for failing to heed God's Word, or more accurately, for failing to yield to God and his rule. While the rulers had been given great power over their subjects, the scope of their authority was sharply limited, or as Luther puts it, "a club is laid beside the dog."[23] God had made the princes "gods" in the temporal realm as the Psalm notes, but God "does not make them gods in such a way as to abolish His own Godhead and let them do as they please, as if they alone were gods over God."[24] Specifically, it is the Word of God, God's self-revelation to his people in Christ and in the recorded Word, the Bible, that serves as the club laid beside the dog. "For God's Word," Luther points out, "appoints them, makes them gods, and subjects everything

22. Ibid., 47.
23. Ibid., 48.
24. Ibid.

10

to them. Therefore they are not to despise it, for it is their institutor and appointer; but they are to be subject to it and allow themselves to be judged, rebuked, made and corrected by it."[25] God's Word is the final authority over all.

Three Princely Virtues

Temporal rulers who embrace their place within God's plan for his creation are distinguished by three notable virtues that Luther finds at least implicitly presented in Psalm 82. The second and third virtues are readily recognizable, and if a list of desirable traits for government officials and leaders were compiled in our day, these two would likely still appear. The first of the pair is "to help the poor, the orphans, and the widows to justice, and to further their cause."[26] While a sizable segment of people in today's Western world would likely applaud Luther's call for princes and governments to serve as champions of the marginalized, others may be somewhat surprised to find the reformer supporting what easily enough could appear to be social welfare. But, this outcome is significantly mitigated when Luther expands his argument and speculates on the best way for a ruler to ensure justice for the less fortunate. This sort of work, Luther believed, was best accomplished when a ruler "makes and preserves just laws."[27] Rather than suggesting a program of taxes to redistribute wealth, Luther calls for rulers to prevent the powerful and influential from fleecing and stealing from those without means. The best remedy for poverty, Luther suggests, is steady justice for all, including the marginalized. Protected by a government's good laws, each person can be safe to pursue his own course in the world without fear. "For so to help a man that he does not need to become a beggar," Luther reasons, "is just as much of a good work and a virtue and an alms as to give to a man and to help a man who has already become a beggar."[28] Good rulers, Luther

25. Ibid.
26. Ibid., 53.
27. Ibid., 54.
28. Ibid.

and all of us agree, should honor and advance justice, especially for the sake of those easily and often abused by the powerful.

The final princely virtue on Luther's list is unlikely to provoke serious objections from any but the most ardent and singular pacifists. "The third virtue," Luther writes, "is that they protect and guard against violence and force. This is called peacemaking."[29] Arms ready to be used against the wicked for the sake of justice and the preservation of peace is, as Luther sees it, one half of the necessary equipment of a good prince. The other half, the second virtue just discussed, is the crafting of laws that advance and guard the practice of justice among all the people. Luther knew that when princes used the sword for the sake of justice and the preservation of peace, all of society reaped countless benefits: "Now, it is from peace that we have our bodies and lives, wives and children, houses and homes, all our members—hands, feet, eyes—and all our health and liberty; and within these walls of peace we sit secure."[30] A prince carrying out the responsibility entrusted to him for the good of his people, including, certainly, the just use of violent force as both threat and even consequence was a great—and rare—blessing from God. Luther acknowledges the necessity of the sword, but is certainly no hawk, and pleads for peace:

> One must not begin a war or work for it; it comes unbidden, all too soon. One must keep peace as long as one can, even though one must buy it with all the money that would be spent on the war or won by the war. Victory never makes up for what is lost by war.[31]

Demonstrating his particular gift as a teacher of the church, Luther's position once again skillfully marries the unyielding ideal of scriptural revelation with the practical pragmatics of concrete reality.

Of all the princely virtues, though, the one of paramount importance, the one that heads Luther's list, is that rulers "can secure justice for those who fear God and repress those who are godless."[32]

---

29. Ibid., 55.
30. Ibid.
31. Ibid., 57.
32. Ibid., 52.

While it would be an easy way out of an awkward situation, in this instance, Luther does not mean "godless" as a mere synonym for unruly, wicked, or rebellious. To be precise, Luther's great hope is that princes would exhibit preferential treatment and support of orthodox Christian teachers and preachers, and pursue a corresponding course of deliberately hampering and even eradicating false teaching. The difficulty, here, is apparent, as most Westerners reflexively recoil from just the sort of ideas being endorsed by Luther. Indeed, their own carefully cultivated sense of enlightenment morality on full display, modern Westerners—"conservative" clergy numbered among them—almost certainly would summarily judge such princely activity not as virtuous but as a capital offense—a violation of the sacrosanct basic human right of religious liberty. But, such alarm at Luther's ardent exhortation for princely solicitude on behalf of orthodox manifestations of the church and her leaders might be somewhat premature. Luther may not offer a stirring defense of an individual's supposed inherent right to believe whatever she may choose; but neither is he interested in compelling belief at the point of a prince's sword. Luther's hope is that princes will recognize the great benefits that come to a nation and its people when the truth of God's Word is clearly taught:

> For if God's Word is protected and supported so that it can be freely taught and learned, and if the sects and false teachers are given no opportunity and are not defended against the teachers who fear God, what greater treasure can there be in a land? Surely God Himself must dwell there, as in His own temple.[33]

As far as Luther is concerned, the obvious civic goods that result from the spread of orthodox teaching warrant the advocacy of such teaching by the prince.

33. Ibid.

Blasphemy and the Duty of a Prince

Aware of the need to clarify his endorsement of princely intervention on behalf of orthodoxy, Luther discusses at some length the extent to which political rulers should work to stop false teaching. Again, his reasoning is grounded in scripture and developed with a pragmatic eye toward real situations. Luther offers four degrees of response, depending on the situation encountered. Beginning with the easiest situation, Luther reminds his readers that many false teachers also stumble into a violation of civil law and order, and so, are to be punished accordingly as mere criminals, regardless of their theological positions. Thinking especially of the enthusiasts who decried all civic authority and even laws regulating private property, Luther did not demur: "These teachers are immediately, and without doubt, to be punished by the rulers, as men who are resisting temporal law and government." The reason was simple and certain. "They are not heretics only," Luther wrote, "but rebels, who are attacking the rulers and their government, just as a thief attacks another's goods, a murderer another's body, an adulterer another's wife; and this is not to be tolerated."[34] Again, based on scripture and practical reason, Luther had no patience for rebellion in any form.

The next possible situation involved teachers who were undermining basic and common Christian confession, such as those who would deny the deity of Christ, or the existence of heaven and hell. In Luther's context, where the nation itself along with its population was Christian by definition, such teaching was more than heresy; it was blasphemy, "and rulers are in duty bound to punish blasphemers as they punish those who curse, swear, revile, abuse, defame, and slander."[35] The practice of blasphemy undermined the fabric of society, and so, was a civic issue. But, in answer to potential critics then and now, Luther did not think that the prosecution of blasphemy was tantamount to a prescribed confession of Christian faith, or a violation

34. Ibid., 61. Among the enthusiasts or "sneak preachers," as Luther sometimes liked to call them, Luther will shortly name Münzer and Carlstadt. Cf. p. 64.
35. Ibid.

of a person's individual will. "By this procedure," Luther reasoned, "no one is compelled to believe, for he can still believe what he will; but he is forbidden to teach and to blaspheme."[36] A person was free to believe what he liked, but was not free to erode or threaten the simple saving faith of the people of the land. Toleration of blasphemy was patently absurd to Luther. Blasphemers "would take from God and the Christians their doctrine and word, and he would do them this injury under their own protection."[37] A blasphemer who could not remain silent about his errant beliefs should "go to some place where there are no Christians."[38] Again, this position was predicated on the assumption that the nation was Christian. In those circumstances, the prosecution of blasphemy is less about religion or doctrine than it is a matter of national identity, unity, and strength. "He who makes a living from the citizens ought to keep the law of the city, and not defame and revile it," Luther insisted, "or else he ought to get out."[39]

A Time for Silence

At this stage of the argument, Luther's own position regarding "religious liberty" was, for his era, rather conventional. When he enters into his third scenario, however, his argument takes a turn that, whether or not surprising, is certainly interesting. The reformer envisions a possibility that requires little imagination. Luther's description, including a reluctant acknowledgment of the rise of *Lutheran* as a label for those committed to orthodoxy as he had revived it, paints a picture readily recognizable by his contemporaries; his recommended action, though, was likely less familiar:

> If it happen that in a parish, a city, or a principality, the papists and the Lutherans (as they are called) are crying out against one another because of certain matters of belief, and preaching against one another, and both parties claim that the Scriptures are on their side, I would not willingly tolerate such a division. My Lutherans ought to be willing to abdicate

36. Ibid., 62.
37. Ibid.
38. Ibid.
39. Ibid.

and be silent if they observed that they were not gladly heard, as Christ teaches.[40]

Citing his own example, Luther implores churchmen to preach, teach, and write only when desired or compelled to do so. The surprising twist is that the one typically deemed as a champion of the declaration of the truth at all costs (the image of the Diet of Worms presents itself easily enough) here advocates a quiescent and even silent manner on the part of the orthodox teacher. For Luther, peace and unity among the people of a place is extremely important: "It is not a good thing that contradictory preaching should go out among the people of the same parish."[41] Luther considered the price of such divisive teaching to be too high, "For from this arise divisions, disorders, hatreds, and envying which extend to temporal affairs also."[42] And in the perhaps inevitable circumstance in which "neither party is willing to yield or be silent, or if neither can do so because of official position," Luther actually turns to the civil rulers to provide a solution: "then let the rulers take a hand."[43] Optimistically, Luther hopes that the rulers would devote time to hear the case and then command silence from the party out of step with the scriptures.

Aside from his startling confidence in the ability of rulers to hear and decide questions of scriptural and theological truth, the reformer's position is noteworthy for at least two other reasons. First, it is significant to see just how permeable was the line of division between the temporal and spiritual realms for Luther. Not only is he comfortable with the state supporting the church, he actually calls on the state to intervene and "rule" in the church when its own leaders are unable to settle matters. But, it must be stressed, such intervention was to be done in conformity with, and in submission to, the norm of scripture, rather than some form of human law or precedent. Luther, it seems, took for granted that rulers in his world would at least be Christian and competent for such judgments. Granting these caveats,

40. Ibid., 62–63.
41. Ibid., 63.
42. Ibid.
43. Ibid.

with his exhortation for princely action on behalf of the church, it is nevertheless clear that Luther's understanding of the "separation of church and state" is altogether different than the one taught in American classrooms and cherished in American hearts.

Second, it is worth noticing Luther's high valuation of civic tranquility manifest in and supported by the uniformity of church doctrine and practice. For the sake of a community's unity and peace, Luther was even willing that those teaching his doctrine should keep silent. Obviously, this appeal cannot be taken in isolation, and should be tempered with Luther's own pleas in other places for steadfast teaching committed to the truth at all costs.[44] And, it must be remembered that while scriptural error is involved in the conflict, Luther can call for silence for the sake of peace, because in this third scenario, the theoretical error did not rise to the level of blasphemy; in other words, perhaps Luther could countenance silence because, as he saw it, salvation was not at stake. Or, maybe more likely still, Luther remained confident—possibly to a fault—that any dispute judged on the basis of scripture could only be decided in favor of the Lutheran position, hence a call for silence was not a serious threat that his own teaching would be muzzled. What should not be missed, however, is the simple truth—that Luther prized peace and unity in the civil realm even at the expense of the free and full proclamation of his own doctrinal position.

Luther's ardent advocacy of civic concord and harmony is further demonstrated when he offers his fourth and final imagined instance of a legitimate civil restriction on religious speech. If scripture is not at stake, "but only ancient custom and man-made law—I mean such questions as tonsures, holy water, the blessing of herbs, and similar unnecessary things," then silence and peace is absolutely mandated.[45] "These wranglings," Luther declares, "are by no means to be tolerated

---

44. One ready example is Luther's short confession that we now call the Smalcald Articles. His preface makes the case for declaring truth in the face of overwhelming opposition, and his final thoughts (SA III, 15, 3) sound a familiar theme: "These are the articles on which I must stand and on which I intend to stand, God willing, until my death. I can neither change nor concede anything in them" (Kolb and Wengert, *The Book of Concord*, 297–300, 326).

45. LW 13, 63.

in the pulpit; but both parties are to be ordered to keep peace."[46] Predictably and quite rightly, Luther insists, that it is, as it always is, scripture alone that must decide the case: "For what the Scriptures do not contain, the preachers ought not wrangle about in the presence of the people."[47] Luther summarizes his thoughts in a statement with axiomatic brevity and force: "for love and peace are far more important than all ceremonies."[48] And for good measure, he then claims the support of St. Paul, "that peace is to be preferred to all else, and it is unchristian to let peace and unity yield to ceremonies."[49] Just how twenty-first-century Christians should apply the reformer's principled call for peace and the required silence of all who would disturb that peace over mere "ceremonies" would likely provoke some lively debate and perhaps even disturb the peace. It is enough, though, for the present purpose to recognize how highly Luther valued order and concord in his community, whether ecclesial and spiritual or civil and temporal.

As far as Luther is concerned, princes acting to curtail false teaching are acting with the highest virtue. Such limits on "free speech" were warranted, Luther was sure, for the sake of the public good—unity in confession and practice shaped and encouraged civil harmony and unity, which were the highest public goods. Clearly, the hegemony of the individual had yet to be established—in spite of the myth, still widespread today, of Luther's complicity in the rise of "personal rights." Further, it is interesting that from the reformer's perspective, none of his restrictions were intended to dictate an individual's particular beliefs or faith. Without equivocation, Luther freely grants, "anyone may read what he likes and believe what he likes."[50] Of course, such willful self-assertion is not without consequences, as Luther makes clear in his next sentence: "If he will not hear God, let him hear the devil."[51] For the good of the people, Luther was certain, the solid

46. Ibid.
47. Ibid.
48. Ibid.
49. Ibid.
50. Ibid., 64.
51. Ibid.

doctrine of scripture was to be preached and instilled into the people of the place, and aberrant teaching was to be silenced. "All this compels no one to believe; but it gives the community peace from the hotheads and puts a stop to the knavery of the fellows who preach in corners, who sneak, uncalled and unsent, into people's houses and emit their poison there before pastors or rulers find them out."[52] Luther's love of order and contempt for the "sneak preachers" is in evidence here, of course, but what is particularly relevant for the present discussion is the natural ease with which Luther places pastors and rulers side by side with the responsibility for rooting out the clandestine false teachers who were probably always the primary target of Luther's calls for silence.

Three Princely Vices

A good ruler, then, practices Luther's three great virtues: "first . . . the furtherance of the Word of God . . . second . . . the administration of just laws . . . third . . . the suppression of violence and the punishment of the wicked."[53] For all of his apparent optimism about the virtuous intervention of a pious prince on behalf of God's people, Luther is hardly naïve about the reality. "These are the virtues they ought to have and practice," Luther writes of the rulers, "But how do things actually go? The very opposite!"[54] With fine rhetorical balance, Luther replaces the three virtues with three vices. Still adamant about the prince's first responsibility for the support of orthodox doctrinal teaching, Luther, nevertheless, is painfully aware of the contrary vice all too common among rulers. "For it is the princes and lords," he declares, "who ought to be advancing God's Word, who do the most to suppress, forbid, and persecute it. Instead, they advance false and injurious teachers."[55] Luther cites Old Testament examples of this sad situation and then offers a general summary: "Therefore, as there is no

52. Ibid.
53. Ibid., 58.
54. Ibid., 59.
55. Ibid.

greater jewel in the world than a God-fearing lord, so there is no more hurtful plague in the world than a godless lord."[56]

Luther recounts a similar breakdown and replacement for the second and third virtues, stemming in both cases from a "spirit of defiance and self-will."[57] Consumed not with the administration of law, but with the acquisition of personal advantage and profit, rulers shun virtue and wallow in vice. After his digression probing the extent to which rulers should intervene in the suppression of heresy, Luther returns to the pestilence of princely vice and provides a succinct list of the three. "The first is that they do not accept the duty of advancing the Word of God."[58] The next vice, negatively mirroring the responsibility of care for the unfortunate, "is that they do not take heed to their secular government and do not provide the poor and wretched with law and protection."[59] The depth of this second vice manifests itself in the sorry fact that rulers not only sin by failing to provide, but actually "vex their subjects with force and wrong, or wink at it when others do so."[60] Finally, the third vice "is that 'they walk in darkness' and in this godless state live only for themselves, as though they had got the rulership in order to seek and pursue only their own profit and honor, their own pleasure and selfish desires, their own pride and pomp, and owed no one either service or help."[61] Though Luther's assessment may lack the pithiness of Lord Acton's famous dictum, the substance is essentially the same. Power tends to corrupt and is far too easily exercised less for the good of the people than for the good of the prince alone.

Obviously, lauding the office of prince while at the same time lamenting the rulers that actually arise creates a certain tension in Luther's teaching. It is not one that should be resolved or diminished. Indeed, any move to settle the question about the godliness and goodness or wickedness and loathsomeness of temporal authority in

56. Ibid., 60.
57. Ibid.
58. Ibid., 68.
59. Ibid., 69.
60. Ibid.
61. Ibid.

a unilateral way—whether deciding in favor of the inherent, and so, unimpeachable divinity and holiness of the office, or surrendering to the bitter reality of man's selfish evil nature, and so, consigning all authority to Satan's domain—is to desert Luther's doctrine and lose the legacy. The beauty and power of Luther's teaching on the two realms of God's reign lie precisely in the maintenance and cultivation of the tension. This truth extends also to the tension involved in calling the prince's office holy and divine, and then, calling the prince himself a self-promoting instrument of hell. For Luther, both statements are fully and concurrently correct and not the least contradictory. "Therefore," Luther asserts, "those estates that are appointed in God's Word are all holy, divine estates, even though the persons in them are not holy."[62] Luther extends the principle well beyond the office of prince or ruler, and subsumes under the teaching all temporal vocations, whether in or under authority: "Thus father, mother, son, daughter, master, mistress, servant, maid, preacher, pastor—all these are holy and divine positions in life, even though the persons in these positions may be knaves and rascals."[63] God establishes the office, but the humans who fill the office inevitably denigrate and disgrace it; such is the tension of the two realms.

The Pastor's Task

Much of what has so far been considered in Luther's commentary on Psalm 82 echoes what he asserts in earlier, more widely read and familiar essays from the 1520s. Indeed, this is precisely one of the important truths to be gained by carefully reading his commentary on Psalm 82: Luther's teaching on the two realms was quite consistent over the span of his career.[64] But, Luther does offer a few exhortations and emphases in this short commentary that are not as prominent in his earlier works, and so, may well be somewhat unfamiliar even to

---

62. Ibid., 71.
63. Ibid.
64. This is the point made quite convincingly in the work by F. Edward Cranz, *An Essay on the Development of Luther's Thought on Justice, Law, and Society* (Mifflintown, PA: Sigler Press, 1987). This essay will be considered more fully in the next chapter.

those who are intent on embracing and following his teaching. The first and probably most interesting and potentially significant of these is his understanding of the pastor's role in speaking necessary guidance, correction, and rebuke to rulers. Of course, Luther is well aware of the unique role and work of a pastor. In fact, in this brief commentary, he makes some rather stirring and even startling assertions with regard to the pastoral office. In the course of making his case for appropriate silence in the name of civil and ecclesial concord, Luther gives a deliberate and categorical direction that is quite remarkable: "This rule should be so rigidly enforced that no preacher, however pious or upright, shall take upon himself either to preach to the people of a papistic or heretical pastor, or to teach them privately, without the knowledge and consent of that pastor."[65] For Luther, the rationale is simple and compelling. "For he has no command to do this," Luther argues, "and what is not commanded should be left undone."[66] At bottom, it is an issue of the office of the holy ministry and the right and responsibility to fill the office. "It is true that all Christians are priests, but not all are pastors. For to be a pastor one must be not only a Christian and a priest but must have an office and a field of work committed to him. This call and command make pastors and preachers."[67] While rulers could, when required, judge intractable disputes among conflicting teachers of doctrine, they were not in the office of pastor. "A burgher or layman may be a learned man; but this does not make him a lecturer and entitle him to teach publicly in the schools or to assume the teaching office [i.e., pastor], unless he is called to it," Luther concludes.[68]

A pastor, then, is unique because his call to serve in the office of the holy ministry places upon him a peculiar burden of responsibility unlike any other. Well aware that his audience would include many who held the pastoral office, even in this brief commentary, Luther

65. *LW* 13, 65.
66. Ibid.
67. Ibid. One gets the sense that much of the bafflement over the nature of the Office and its relation to the "priesthood of believers" that seems to confound so many in the church would be rather deftly handled and undone by the reformer himself were he to enter the fray today.
68. Ibid.

manages to provide a rather comprehensive and ambitious description of this pastoral responsibility. It is worth hearing him in full as he contrasts the glitz and show of great churches and lavish ornamentation with the humble presence of a faithful pastor:

> Meanwhile my pastor, who does not glitter, is practicing the virtue that increases God's kingdom, fills heaven with saints, plunders hell, robs the devil, wards off death, represses sin, instructs and comforts every man in the world according to his station in life, preserves peace and unity, raises fine young folk, and plants all kinds of virtue in the people. In a word, he is making a new world! He builds not a poor, temporary house, but an eternal and beautiful Paradise, in which God Himself is glad to dwell.[69]

purpose of preaching

Of course, Luther was not foolish enough to think that all who held the office would adequately fulfill their work. The disjunction between the divine role and the broken practitioner of that role held as much in the ecclesial realm as it did in the temporal. Luther's lament has a timeless ring: "Would God that only faithful men had this office and administered it faithfully and purely, and that it were not abused so shamefully and hatefully! Nevertheless, abuse does not destroy the office; the office is true exactly as temporal rule is a true and good office, even though a knave has it and abuses it."[70] There was no exception or exemption. The truth of God's Word and the truth of hard reality both held firmly in both realms.

While it is not the focus of the present study, it is worth noting in passing that as Luther details the tasks of a pastor, he obviously understands that such work is not limited solely to matters impacting the vertical relationship between people and God. Not atypically, Luther also recognizes and endorses the need for a pastor to address areas important in the horizontal relationships of life in the world. In short, it is not enough that people know they are forgiven and will spend an eternity with Christ; they must also be equipped to be "fine young folk" outfitted with "all kinds of virtue." And a pastor's sincere and apposite concern for the good of the temporal world with its many

69. Ibid., 52–53.
70. Ibid., 49.

vocations, responsibilities, and demanding relationships includes in addition a concern for the vocation of ruler and the virtues or lack of virtues of the one currently assigned to that vocation. Every ruler is accountable to the will and word of God, and that will and word of God are delivered to the ruler through the pastor. Expounding upon the first verse of Psalm 82, Luther is quite sure that God "stands" and "judges" in the midst of the congregation through "His appointed priests and preachers."[71] Through his chosen pastor, God speaks his Word to his people. Luther seems to take for granted that the prince actually would be present among the people of a congregation so that the pastor could deliver God's Word to him. Perhaps in sixteenth-century Germany, this was the case; while hardly a safe assumption, today, it matters little for the point I intend to make.

Pastor vs. Prince

Throughout the commentary, Luther adopts the nomenclature of the psalm and refers to princes and rulers as "gods." The preacher, then, speaks God's Word to the gods:

> Observe, however, that a preacher by whom God rebukes the gods is to "stand in the congregation." He is to "stand": that is, he is to be firm and confident and deal uprightly and honestly with it; and "in the congregation," that is, openly and boldly before God and men. By this two sins are prevented.[72]

Unfaithfulness, seen when pastors "lie down or otherwise play with their office," is the first sin that is avoided. The majority of the time, Luther believes, such unfaithfulness is manifest in "lazy and worthless preachers who do not tell the princes and lords their sins."[73] But, there are also those obsequious pastors who pander to princes; they "play the hypocrite and flatter the wicked gods and strengthen them in their self-will."[74] The other sin, Luther calls backbiting. "The whole world,"

71. Ibid.
72. Ibid.
73. Ibid.
74. Ibid.

Luther complains, "is full in every corner of preachers and laymen who bandy evil words about their gods, i.e., princes and lords, curse them, and call them names, though not boldly in the open, but in corners and in their own sects."[75] This sin yields civic disaster, kindling a "secret fire by which people are moved to disobedience, rebellion, breach of the peace, and contempt for their rulers."[76] This fire was not unfamiliar to Luther—the ashes of the peasant's revolt still smoldered around him. Five hundred years later, the fire continues to be lit by pastors who speak of their own "rulers" with an eye-roll, an arched eyebrow, a sneer, or outright ridicule and disdain. Luther speaks stern words of his own to such pastors: "If you are in the ministry and are not willing to rebuke your gods openly and publicly, as your office demands, at least leave off your private backbiting, calling of names, criticizing, and complaining, or go hang!"[77] Indeed.

There are, of course, elements of Luther's argument in his commentary that are context-specific and not immediately relevant in the twenty-first century. Princes do not ordinarily occupy our pews and power hungry monks do not pose a problem for many congregations. But, the force of Luther's argument is absolutely relevant, and I believe, seldom heard, much less understood and practiced in our day. Consider again the foundational assumption undergirding Luther's discussion about faithful pastors. It is a given for the reformer that a pastor would guide and rebuke a prince as necessary. This is extraordinary—that is, from a typical separation-of-church-and-state-perspective, the notion of a preacher calling out a ruler and rebuking him is probably more than a bit disconcerting. Yet, this is exactly what Luther has in mind. God does not tolerate the secret judging that fuels backbiting, Luther insists. "On the other hand," he continues, it is His will that those who are in office [of the Ministry] and are called to do so shall rebuke and judge their gods boldly and

75. Ibid.
76. Ibid., 50.
77. Ibid.

openly."[78] Not content to make his point once, Luther elaborates at length:

> So, then, this first verse teaches that to rebuke rulers is not seditious, provided it is done in the way here described; namely, by the office to which God has committed that duty, and through God's Word, spoken publicly, boldly, and honestly. To rebuke rulers in this way is, on the contrary a praiseworthy, noble, and rare virtue, and a particularly great service to God, as the psalm here proves. It would be far more seditious if a preacher did not rebuke the sins of the rulers; for then he makes people angry and sullen, strengthens the wickedness of the tyrants, becomes a partaker in it, and bears responsibility for it. Thus God might be angered and allow rebellion to come as a penalty. The other way—when the lords are rebuked as well as the people, and the people as well as the lords (as the prophets did)—no one can blame anything on the other person. They have to bear with one another, be satisfied, and be at peace with one another.[79]

It is important to recognize that it is the sins of a lord as lord that are to be rebuked, and not merely the general shortcomings common to all fallen humans. In other words, Luther envisions a pastor naming the sins peculiar to a lord, just as he names the sins peculiar to a peasant. "For a preacher," continues Luther, "is neither a courtier nor a hired hand. He is God's servant and slave, and his commission is over lords and slaves."[80] The ruler's high office does not exempt him from the judgment of God's Word delivered through the mouth of the pastor. Neither does the prince's office in the temporal realm remove his actions there from review and criticism by the spiritual realm.

Reading and thinking with Luther, it is easy to consider the crux of this argument as all but self-evident, and to accept it as effortlessly and thoughtlessly as Luther seems to assume it. It is important, then, to linger for just a moment, and contemplate, however incipiently, the import and potential implications of Luther's position. If Luther is right, then would it not be altogether appropriate for a pastor to denounce from the pulpit the city's US congressman for his floor vote

78. Ibid.
79. Ibid., 50–51.
80. Ibid., 51.

26

that violated God's Law? If Luther is right, then would not the state governor's advocacy for a policy that opposed God's clear Word be subject to public reprimand by God's preacher? If Luther is right, then should not those charged with the responsibility to elect their rulers be instructed by the pastor about the moral implications of a vote? If Luther is right about the responsibility of a pastor to rebuke a prince, there is, I suspect, a fair amount of adjustment to be made in the way that many American Christians have come to understand the appropriate role of a pastor vis-à-vis the government. Obviously, more needs to be said, and caveats and rejoinders need to be addressed, but that will come in time. To fulfill the task of the present chapter, it is enough to make sure that Luther is being heard all the way—even, indeed especially, when what Luther says confronts and challenges long-held assumptions or cherished opinions.

The Problem of Misuse and Misapplication

The stark simplicity and compelling force of Luther's argument often engenders a measure of anxiety. An immediate and understandable concern that asserts itself is the possible abuse of the teaching. Is it not possible that a pastor could become consumed with politics and the gospel's proclamation be eclipsed? Could it be that a prince would claim the divinity of his office as license for great wickedness? Might a nation of believers be lulled into quietism and inaction by their wrong understanding of the distinction between the two realms? None of these concerns is idle fancy. All have been realized in history. So, who is to blame? To quell the inevitable abuse, must Luther's teaching be modified, damped, or discarded altogether? Of course, since Luther's day, there have been those who have, with varying intensity, answered in the affirmative.

Luther himself was already aware of the charge. It was widely recognized at the time, even by the reformer himself, that Lutheran teaching had played at least some role in the disturbance that mushroomed into the disaster called the Peasant's Revolt. It is hardly unexpected then, that Luther addresses the problem of misapplied teaching in his commentary. "Perhaps someone may give me another clever answer," suggests Luther, "and say that with this kind of teaching [specifically, the call for rulers to punish blasphemers] I am strengthening the case of the tyrants who persecute the Gospel and am opening door and window for them."[81] The fear, not without reason, was that rulers "who consider our Gospel heresy and blasphemy" would actually use the mandate to punish the Lutherans as blasphemers. Luther is unmoved. "What do I care?" he retorts, "If we were to hold back necessary instruction because of the tyrants, we would long since have had to give up the Gospel altogether."[82] For Luther, there is nothing to discuss: scripture is clear, and faithful doctrine must follow suit, regardless of the price. Luther admits that even the kings of Israel had killed true prophets. "Nevertheless," he concludes, "we must not abolish or hide the commandment to stone false prophets; but pious rulers will punish no man without first seeing, hearing, learning, and becoming certain that he is a blasphemer."[83] Luther may be right about pious rulers, but by his own admission, these were rare.

Actually, the actions of a ruler—pious or otherwise—are irrelevant to Luther's argument. His central point is simply that a faithful teacher must teach what he has been given to teach by his Lord. The pragmatics and practical consequences of ideas may be significant for politicians, public policy gurus, and health care workers, but they cannot dictate doctrinal truth or teaching. Luther knew this, and his dismissive attitude toward those who worried about the possible consequences of teaching forthrightly about a ruler's responsibility to quash blasphemy is consistent with a wider principle. The truth is the truth, and must be taught even if it is misunderstood, misapplied, or otherwise abused. Never is this truer than in the work of theology. Obviously, of course, sloppy, inept, inaccurate, or careless teaching is never excused, and bears its own consequences. But not even rebelling peasants, self-indulgent rulers, or apathetic citizens can be cited as just

81. Ibid., 67.
82. Ibid.
83. Ibid.

cause to alter the forthright teaching of God's truth. Faithful teaching must profess the truth of God's Word as it is given. Luther applied the principle with great consistency. Understanding the importance of this dictum for Luther is essential for making sense of Luther's positions on various social issues that may otherwise appear erratic or even arbitrary.

Come, Lord Jesus!

The final verse of Psalm 82 is a fitting petition: "Arise, O God, judge the earth! For it is You who possesses all the nations." The prayer inspires Luther to conclude his thoughts on the Psalm with an impassioned proclamation of the gospel of Jesus quite in character for the reformer. For Luther, the prayer points directly to a fulfillment in the coming of Christ. Luther again voices his pessimism and ultimate despair over the "godhead" of temporal rulers: "Worldly government will make no progress. The people are too wicked, and the lords dishonor God's name and Word continually by the shameful abuse of their godhead."[84] So, the true God himself must come and accomplish the work of faithful ruling and judging that must be done but is left utterly undone by those entrusted with the task. So, Christ comes. He establishes "another government and kingdom in which things will be better, where God's name will be honored, His Word kept and He Himself be served."[85] Luther seems to equate this government with the spiritual realm in which the pastor and the church particularly operate in ways that correspond to the role of ruler and government in the temporal realm. "This is the kingdom of Jesus Christ," he asserts, "this is the true God, who has come and is judging."[86] As Luther unfolds his soaring description of Christ's rule, he makes clear that Jesus eclipses and supplants the failed rulers of the worldly government:

> For Christ practices aright the three divine virtues mentioned above. He advances God's Word and the preachers of it; He makes and keeps law

---

84. Ibid., 72.
85. Ibid.
86. Ibid.

for the poor; He protects and rescues the miserable. The service of God in Christendom is justice, peace, righteousness, life, salvation. Of this kingdom of Christ the Gospels, and the Epistles of the apostles, preach and testify so fully that there is no need to speak further of them here.[87]

What earthly rulers in the temporal realm would not and could not do, Jesus does perfectly.

Luther's unqualified praise of Christ's supremacy aligns so seamlessly with Christian confession and piety that it is startlingly easy to pass over his concluding thoughts without reflection. Of course, Jesus is the ultimate and ideal lord. Of course, he accomplishes all that temporal lords could not. Of course, his kingdom is superior to all earthly kingdoms and dominions. There is nothing here that counters or challenges Christian faith. As Luther drives to the final words of the essay, the doxology swells: *look to Jesus to do the 3 as this rule is eternal, unlike the rule of govt.*

Thus we see that, over and above the righteousness, wisdom, and power of this world, there is another righteousness, wisdom, and power. For the righteousness of this world has an end, but the righteousness of Christ and of those who are in His kingdom abides forever. To this may He help us and keep us, who is our King, our dear Lord and God, Jesus Christ. May He, with the Father and the Holy Ghost in one essential and eternal Godhead, be praised and blessed forever. Amen.

Between the temporal kingdoms and finite power of this world, and the eternal kingdom and infinite power of Christ, there is, of course, no comparison. Luther's reminder of Christ's ultimate triumph over all trivial human pretension and silly mortal posturing speaks truth and speaks it with perfect timing as an apt denouement to the entire commentary.

A Problem and a Solution

To raise any objection to Luther's final pious words of prayer and praise would seem ridiculously imprudent. Even so, the stark contrast between worldly righteousness, wisdom, and power and Christ's greater kingdom with its own superior righteousness, wisdom, and

87. Ibid.

power could introduce a troublesome wrinkle in the otherwise tightly woven material of Luther's commentary. The final lopsided contrast between the earthly kingdoms and Christ's kingdom seems to refute all that previously had been said about the temporal realm as God's own important and necessary realm. If the world's kingdoms are pathetic and worthless after all, then lofty talk of the vital and holy work of temporal rulers and governments seems feigned and insincere, or just deceitful. And even if this wrinkle is ironed out with some deft and probably appropriate eschatological special pleading, there remains the problem of the relation between the glorious kingdom of Christ described by Luther here and the spiritual realm of God's activity introduced earlier. Christ's kingdom, Christians confess, is not just coming, but is present in the Word and work of the church today. Does that mean, then, that the spiritual domain present now in the church as it lives out the Gospel narrative is the same thing as Christ's kingdom lauded by Luther? And, if that is the case, then, does that not mean that the temporal realm is, in reality, woefully inferior to the spiritual, and actually the only realm that matters is the spiritual? It is not hard to imagine Luther's final words adding credence to the thinking—not unheard of in the church—that all human governments and rulers are always suspect and inherently unholy, and so, not deserving of the genuine attention and effort of good Christian people.

The teaching of the two realms of God's activity in the world hinges on two realms operating side by side, both instituted and directed by God and both administered by fallen and fallible human creatures placed in their offices by God. Neither is over the other. Both play a critical role in God's plan for this world; both are doing God's work; both matter to God, and so, should matter to his people; both are good. How to maintain and honor that duality while also finding a way faithfully to confess the indisputable truth of Christ's kingdom triumphant over all, as Luther does so fluently at the conclusion of his commentary, is a question that deserves an answer. Indeed, without a satisfactory solution to the problem, the stability and credibility of the two realms model is seriously, if not fatally, challenged: the temporal *where the sinful gird fails, the orthodox pastor must bring to light by returning to Christ's rule*

realm withers into inconsequence. Still, this is not Luther's immediate concern here, and he can hardly be faulted for failing to acknowledge or appreciate the issue. The predicament is certainly not readily apparent. Christian truth and piety are quite enough to obscure the difficulty. Whatever the reason, the reformer is content to teach the two coextensive and mutually supportive realms of God's activity, the temporal and the spiritual; and to assert with complete conviction the unmitigated supremacy of Christ's kingdom. Luther does not answer a question he does not raise, but a solution consistent with his teaching is at hand, and the dilemma is not as dramatic as portrayed. Following the course hinted at in the previous paragraph, the resolution to the problem lies in recognizing both the fulfillment and the disjunction of the eschatological consummation.

Christ's coming impacts the entire creation, bringing all of it to its intended wholeness. All things are restored and brought at last into full and breathtaking conformity with God's eternal plan. At the eschatological fulfillment, there will be continuity with all that is now seen and known in the world, yet there will also be discontinuity. In the fullness of Christ's unveiled glory, the new will so expand and excel what is present that it may well be all but unrecognizable. Of course, it is wise to exercise restraint in asserting too much, lest speculation replace revelation. The experience of such things lies ahead for us all. Still, the scriptural indications of the approaching reality support this understanding of continuity coupled with disjunction. In the closing paragraphs of his commentary, Luther celebrates the surpassing greatness of Christ's coming kingdom, and the discontinuity with all fallible earthly powers. This is quite right. All worldly power and authority will be trumped and overwhelmed at the final coronation of God's messiah. Luther emphasizes the surpassing of temporal powers, but it will also be spiritual powers that are swallowed up and eclipsed on the last day. Peopled with fallen creatures, the structures and leaders of the spiritual realm are also in need of restoration. In the reality of the fallen creation in which we all live and move, all institutions and all leaders are fraught with foibles and failings and flat-out wickedness. What is true of temporal princes is also true of spiritual pastors. At his coming, Christ transcends both realms, reunites them under his naked sovereignty, and manifests for all to see the singular beauty of authority and dominion in perfect conformity with God's eternal plan for his creation. Such exercise of authority is nowhere present in the creation as we now experience it—not in the halls of civil government, and not in the sanctuaries of the church. The eschaton will accentuate the disjunction between Christ's perfect authority and rule and the broken authority and rule of this present age.

With the disjunction, however, there will also be continuity with what is. The spiritual realm, though shot through with sin and its consequences as it is administered, is Christ's realm even now. In the spiritual realm, in the church, Christ works and accomplishes his purposes through and even in spite of imperfect human instruments. So, Christ's spiritual or right-hand reign will be brought to completion and fullness at the second coming. But, so also will the temporal or left-hand realm be brought to its completion and fullness. The critical point, once again, is the recognition of the temporal realm and authority as belonging fully to God and operating under his control and according to his purposes. It is helpful to remember that even unbelieving Cyrus was God's chosen instrument, his messiah, and that all human government, including imperial Rome, functioned under God's authority, even when the office-holders were oblivious of the reality. When Christ comes in glory, temporal authority will not be summarily trampled and vanquished, but like spiritual authority, brought to its intended fullness and wholeness. Both realms will be redeemed and restored according to God's design. Of course, since the right-hand or spiritual realm today is charged to speak much more directly and intentionally for Christ and delivers the eternal righteousness of the gospel, it is no doubt easier to see the continuity there, than it is with today's sword-wielding realm of God's left hand.[88]

---

88. Luther's distinction between the two kinds of righteousness—one earthly, horizontal, and actively pursued by creatures; the other spiritual, vertical, and passively received through faith in Christ—is certainly at work, here, and tends to complicate the clarity of the overall argument.

Admittedly, Luther does not provide the sort of neat packaging of the two realms and Christ's eschatological fulfillment that I have attempted. I am confident, however, that what I have offered as a solution to the problem of the superiority of Christ's kingdom over all worldly kingdoms is consistent with Luther's thought, and could garner his endorsement.

The Legacy of Luther

Raising the issue of a possible incongruity in Luther's argument has served a dual purpose. Not only has it offered an honest reading of Luther's commentary—even when that reading appeared unfavorable to the thesis, but it has also allowed a concise presentation of the essence of Luther's concept of the two realms. It should be clear by now that while Luther's foundational idea is deceptively simple and easy to state, the application of the teaching and the practice of the two realms can quickly become bewilderingly complex. In this world, God has determined to execute his will through two distinct avenues or realms. The temporal realm focuses on the preservation of this world and the promotion of peace and justice within it. The spiritual realm centers on the proclamation of the gospel and the delivery of justifying grace. In the temporal realm, God does his work through government and princes. In the spiritual realm, the work is carried out through the church and her pastors. Princes do have a responsibility for spiritual concerns, including the suppression of blasphemy. Pastors do have an obligation to the civil realm, even rebuking princes who defy God's law. Both pastors and princes are God's appointed servants,

When he writes, "For the righteousness of this world has an end, but the righteousness of Christ and of those who are in His kingdom abides forever," Luther is contrasting these two kinds of righteousness (ibid.). In one sense, from the eternal perspective of one's standing before God, vertical righteousness is absolutely superior. That this is the righteousness delivered in the spiritual realm of the church seems to underwrite the superiority of that realm. But, in the reality of life lived in this creation, horizontal righteousness has its rightful place and reasserts itself over vertical righteousness (c.f. Luther's discussion of chapter 2 verse 14 in his Great Galatians commentary, LW 26, 115-17: "There [in society] let nothing be known about the Gospel, conscience, grace, the forgiveness of sins, heavenly righteousness, or Christ Himself; but let there be knowledge only of Moses, of the Law and its works," 116). Thus, in the context of the present state of creation, it is never prudent to suggest the superiority or triumph of one realm over the other.

but both pastors and princes are fallen human beings and sadly capable of incompetence, sloppy dereliction of duty, and even great evil. In Christ, God's kingdom will triumph over all fallen human rule, yet Christ's kingdom will fulfill and complete all that God has accomplished through those same fallen structures and rulers. This is the dynamic and powerful tool of Luther's two realms. Its importance for rightly understanding the world cannot be overemphasized. Its capacity for clarifying and directing the thinking and acting of God's people is virtually without limit.

2

The Two Realms: Interpreters of Luther, Faithful and Otherwise

No one thinks in a vacuum and no one writes in a vacuum. Our upbringing, education, confession, experiences, relationships, and aspirations form an impossibly complex matrix of influences, assumptions, and instruments (both assets and liabilities), which shape and direct all that we think, believe, teach, and write. This is all patently true and not the least insightful, but it also means that there was a definite impetus behind this book beyond the simple expectations of life in the academy. One of the motivations was what I perceived to be a basic need for a text that would explicate Luther's teaching on the two realms accurately, and then provide some concrete and unambiguous assertions about how it would look if this teaching were faithfully applied in the contemporary Western—or more specifically, American—context. Asked on countless occasions to recommend a "good book" on the two kingdoms, I often struggled to name one that did not come with a list of caveats.[1] The other, and

---

1. There are, as I hope to acknowledge and honor as this chapter unfolds, a number of faithful

certainly related, precipitating concern was my perception—or more honestly, my assumption—that much of what had been written on the subject of the two realms was just plain wrong. The attitudes, ideas, and practices I encountered in seminary classroom discussions, church Bible studies, and pastoral conferences within my Lutheran orbit were staunchly held and unwaveringly consistent: the "two kingdoms doctrine" was essentially a Lutheran label for the rigorous and radical separation of church and state as generally articulated and practiced in American society. More than a benign oversimplification of Luther's teaching, this pervasive belief is—I hope, now becoming clear—dangerously wrong and also detrimental to Christian discipleship, the mission of the church, and the world's obligation to advance justice. Since such widely distributed ideas do not arise spontaneously, it seemed safe to conclude that the teaching behind the thinking must be deficient. In other words, the books and articles that had formed the thinking of the church's pastors and people were to blame. My hope was to right the wrong—or at least, to nudge the discussion in a more faithful and more productive direction.

In an effort to find the source or sources of the errant understanding of the two realms, I began reading in earnest. It turned out that I was wrong. Well, not entirely. There is, to be sure, material that perpetuates the overly simplistic divide between the realms and that tends to diminish the value or merit of the temporal domain. But, to my pleasant surprise, I discovered that over the course of the last few generations, a notable number of theologians have faithfully preserved the core of Luther's teaching and some have gone further still and offered carefully considered and appropriate recommendations for practicing the teaching in the modern world. While a solid theological and academic pedigree of two realms thinking is an unexpected boon, it also prompts an unexpected array of perplexing questions related

---

and exceptionally helpful books and essays that have been of great benefit to me, of course. But for the purposes of recommendation to a student or Bible class participant who needed an unvarnished and uncomplicated presentation, the books that came to mind frequently seemed to be too dated, too complicated, too preoccupied with a particular agenda, overly subtle or timid in their presentation, or too distracted by divergent theses to be recommended without hesitation.

to ecclesiastical education, transmission of doctrine, influences on theological thinking, and the forces that form opinion. How can there be such a yawning breach between the largely faithful and worthwhile written legacy devoted to the teaching of the two realms and the sadly defective and damaging ideas widely held by the supposed heirs of that legacy? Interesting and important as they are, such questions lie well outside the scope of the task at hand and are perhaps better left to students of sociology and pedagogy anyway. For now, it is enough to offer a quick sampling from the inheritance that is available.

This chapter is not an account of the history of the doctrine, or even a brief overview of the progression of two realms thinking since Luther. Much more modest, my goal is merely to highlight some of the more valuable resources from the last several decades and hopefully promote a renewed interest in a treasure that has been woefully neglected. I make no pretense of being exhaustive, and will no doubt commit my own sins of neglect and oversight. I believe, though, that there is great value in recognizing the depth of careful thinking that has been devoted to the topic of the two realms, and even a cursory reading can accomplish this. Before turning to that, however, fairness requires, at minimum, a brief account of some material that, from my perspective, is less than helpful and substantiates my earlier charge of a pervasive and malign misconstrual of Luther's teaching.

Holding the Realms at Arm's Length

Generations of Lutheran pastors in my own denomination, the Lutheran Church Missouri Synod, were taught the rudiments of their theological confession by Francis Pieper. The lectures that formed his text, *Christian Dogmatics*, were delivered in German in the second and third decades of the twentieth century, translated into English, and then, printed and reprinted until the present. The three volumes comprise more than 1600 pages, eight of which address issues relating to the two realms. Actually, it is interesting that the venerable professor of systematic theology did not devote a discreet chapter, section, or even subsection specifically to the question of the spiritual and the temporal realms. Instead, he distributes the discussion over two different places, one within an exposition of the means of grace, the other in a section on the church's foundation and preservation. The heart of the argument in both sections seems to be that the government should never be used to accomplish the work of the church. Pieper sums up his thinking in one place by insisting, "we must be content with these means [of grace] and refrain from employing the powers of the State to build the Church."[2] Pieper's point, in this case, aimed true to form at the Reformed, is correct and well taken. Yet, Pieper himself seems somewhat perturbed by the unfortunate willingness to use the state in support of the church by no one less than Luther himself. After lamenting that "the mingling of Church and State, sad to say, crept into the Lutheran Church, too," Pieper raises the problem of Luther in a footnote: "Subject to historical investigation is the question whether Luther did not in specific cases transgress the correct principle taught by him. Such a thing happens also to eminent people."[3] Calling Luther's use of state support "his accommodation to the prevailing confused conditions" is the extent of Pieper's criticism, but it is clear that he is disappointed that he cannot cite Luther's behavior in support of his own principled separation of church and state.

While it is certainly possible that "eminent people" will, from time to time, fall short of their own dictums and will stray from the path of their own teaching, accusing Luther of transgressing his teaching on the two realms, is dubious at best. Luther's perceived infraction was hardly anomalous, isolated, or the fruit of momentary weakness. Rather than blaming Luther for inconsistency, it seems both more reasonable and more just to blame the interpreter for deriving and enforcing the wrong principle. Luther's spirit of cooperation and even mutual support with regard to the princes of his time certainly violates the American principle of separation of church and state, but is actually quite in keeping with his own teaching. Pieper's inability to

2. Francis Pieper, *Christian Dogmatics* (St. Louis, MO: Concordia, 1953), 183.
3. Ibid., 182.

accept and appreciate Luther's actions in relation to the state evidences the great dogmatician's wooden understanding of the divide between the realms. And Pieper's abiding influence on contemporary Lutheran pastors and their flocks may help account for a similar lack of dynamism in the application of the teaching of the two realms in today's Lutheran congregations.

Several generations later, another faithful theologian from the Missouri Synod, Kurt Marquart, reiterated the same ultimately dismissive attitude toward the temporal realm. In the midst of an otherwise insightful and compelling study of church and ministry, Marquart briefly addresses and recognizes the legitimate work of the left-hand realm. But, his concluding thoughts on the subject feature an unfortunate comment that, whether intentional or not, certainly diminishes the temporal realm: "All this [rulers or governments], however, is secondary, provisional, ancillary, penultimate. The whole 'Left Hand' Kingdom is but a vast scaffolding for God's ultimate purpose: the eternal salvation of His church."[4] While it is quite true that the church is God's chosen bride, it is certainly not true that the material world with its guardian, the state, is mere scaffolding for what actually counts, or that it will be excluded from a place in the eschatological consummation. Whatever Marquart may have believed or taught, unfortunately, the message here is that the temporal realm does not finally matter.

In 1998, Daniel Deutschlander, who taught at Martin Luther College in New Ulm, Minnesota, published a book with the promising title, *Civil Government: God's Other Kingdom*. There is much that is good and useful in the book, but what is positive is overshadowed by the underlying attitude pervasive throughout the text that "God's other kingdom" is not a gift to be celebrated, but a regrettable reality to be endured. For Deutschlander, the divide between the two kingdoms is sharp, easily determined, and decidedly imbalanced, with the spiritual trumping the material in every way:

---

4. Kurt Marquart, *The Church and Her Fellowship, Ministry, and Governance* (Fort Wayne, IN: The International Foundation for Lutheran Confessional Research, 1990), 176.

> The gospel for the church; the sword for the state. Hearts and souls for the church; outward behavior for the state. Eternal life with this life as a pilgrimage for the church; temporal matters and this life as the sole concern for the state. That should be sufficient to keep the church as the church out of the Christian right and the Christian left political movements.[5]

Consistent with this posture, the author confidently states an axiom that has become commonplace in virtually every Lutheran discussion of the two realms. "The church has no business telling the voter how to vote. That is the business of Christians *as citizens*," Deutschlander insists, "not the business of the church."[6] As far as the professor from the Wisconsin Synod is concerned, it is all cut and dried: "The church is there to educate Christians from the Word of God for time and for eternity. Christians do not need the church to do their thinking for them in applying the Word of God to specific candidates for public office."[7] In this way of thinking, a separation of church and state necessitates a church that stays out of all politics—even the political thoughts of its own members.

The absolute proscription forbidding the church—presumably the church's pastor or other leaders, are chiefly in mind—from ever daring to "tell a Christian how to vote" enjoys wide circulation well beyond the borders of the WELS. In 2015, the LCMS journal, *The Lutheran Witness*, dedicated an entire issue to questions of church and state. The issue included a full-page chart summarizing what one needs to know about "Christ and Caesar: Being a Christian Citizen."[8] First, the right actions of church and state are delineated. The church is to "Preach the Word of God and administer the Holy Sacraments" while the state is to "Restrain and punish evildoers and commend those who do good."[9] The scriptural foundation for these assertions is apparent. Less apparent is the scriptural support for the subsequent negative

5. Daniel M. Deutschlander, *Civil Government: God's Other Kingdom* (Milwaukee, WI: Northwestern, 1998), 201.
6. Ibid., 194 (italics in original).
7. Ibid.
8. *The Lutheran Witness* 134, no. 1 (Jan 2015): 15.
9. Ibid.

assertions. According to the chart, there are three things that the church "doesn't do." It does not "endorse candidates," or "tell members how to vote," or "make partisan political statements."[10] So familiar and comfortable is this refrain bracketing the church out of "politics" that the enormous assumptions and interpretations that must be at work between what is stated in scripture and what is merely inferred operate unnoticed. It is one thing to affirm the church's sacred primary task of delivering the gospel. It is something else altogether to assert that in a democratic republic, the church can say nothing specific to people about their exercise of the franchise. One must be careful to recognize the ideas and thinking that actually form and support the conclusions that are reached. In the case of the old adage forbidding any ecclesial instruction touching partisan politics or voting choices, it is far easier to see the influence of Thomas Jefferson than to discern the thought of Martin Luther.

Luther "Discovered" by the Reformed?

The early twenty-first century has witnessed a renewed interest in the teaching of Luther not only among Lutherans, but also among some Lutheran cousins. An assortment of Calvinist leaders gives evidence, sometimes by open admission, of influence by Lutheran thinkers and Lutheran ideas. As expected, this turn has been greeted both with applause and with alarm. In 2010, a professor at Westminster Seminary, David VanDrunen, published *Living in God's Two Kingdoms*, in which he makes a case for his understanding of the two realms.[11] Marshaling Augustine, Luther, and Calvin to his side, VanDrunen claims their mantle: "This book, in developing a contemporary and biblically-based two-kingdoms doctrine, follows this Augustinian and Reformation trajectory."[12] Perhaps VanDrunen's trajectory can be traced to some parts of the Reformation, but his vision of the two kingdoms clearly does not cohere with the one taught by Luther.

10. Ibid.
11. David VanDrunen, *Living in God's Two Kingdoms: A Biblical Vision for Christianity and Culture* (Wheaton, IL: Crossway, 2010).
12. Ibid., 25.

VanDrunen's two kingdoms are the "common kingdom" and the "redemptive kingdom," corresponding in good Calvinist fashion to the distinction between covenants with Noah and Abraham, respectively.[13] Without even broaching the rather bizarre concept traced by the author of the "world-to-come" that was to be man's final home, had Adam successfully navigated the "probationary period" of Eden, there is much in VanDrunen's work that should cause concern. Much as he tries to quell the charge, VanDrunen's position ultimately advances the argument that this temporal world does not finally matter. "As they live in two kingdoms, however," VanDrunen contends, "Christians must remember that only one of these kingdoms is destined to endure. They live in the common kingdom as sojourners and exiles, waiting eagerly for Christ, the last Adam, to return and to usher in his redemptive kingdom in the fullness of its glory."[14] Of course, there is truth here; but there is also a patronizing tolerance of the temporal realm that does not cohere with Luther's own teaching and practice. Just as Calvinism can only suggest obedience as a reason for practicing the sacraments—gutted as they are of anything more than symbolic value—VanDrunen can only point to God's command as reason for investing in this passing world:

> The Lord Jesus, as a human being—as the last Adam—has attained the original goal held out for Adam: a glorified life ruling the world-to-come. Because Jesus has fulfilled the first Adam's commission, those who belong to Christ by faith are no longer given that commission. Christians already possess eternal life and claim an everlasting inheritance. God does not call them to engage in cultural labors so as to earn their place in the world-to-come. We are not little Adams. Instead, God gives us a share in the world-to-come as a gift of free grace in Christ and then calls us to live obediently in this world as a grateful response.[15]

VanDrunen is quite right, of course, about a person's works having nothing to do with personal salvation. But his odd understanding of

13. Ibid., 76.
14. Ibid., 128.
15. Ibid., 28.

Adam fuels an attitude toward the world than cannot help but encourage an ultimate assessment that is disdainful and disparaging.

In his final arguments, VanDrunen's scorn for the present world becomes more evident. As Christians, he argues, "we conduct ourselves as sojourners and exiles who share them [activities of *this world* and the affairs of the *common kingdom*] in common with unbelievers and do not really feel at home when pursuing them."[16] Christians, it seems, know better than to exhibit or experience any real sense of affinity with this passing world. "Whatever contributions we make, small or great, are contributions to a cultural arena that is temporary and fleeting."[17] It seems that in VanDrunen's world-to-come, there will be no Bach cantatas, Cranach woodcuts, or Michelangelo sculptures. Inevitably, even Christian vocations are also tempered and truncated. "Many authors," notes VanDrunen, "speak about the Christian's vocation as 'holy' or 'sacred' and claim that God 'redeems' it. But while *Christians themselves* are holy and redeemed, as citizens of the redemptive kingdom, their daily vocations are not." The reason is obvious: "They labor in the things of *this present world*, things that are fleeting."[18] Considering the internecine assaults on thinkers such as VanDrunen, it would be preferable to offer support to those who are at least reading Luther. But while the study and appropriation of Luther always deserves hearty support, one cannot blindly applaud the mere invocation of the Wittenberg reformer when the doctrine that is actually taught emerges as a distortion of Luther.

Not a New Problem, but an American One

Getting Luther right often proves quite challenging—and never more, it seems, than with the question of the two realms. This is not to say that Luther is the final arbiter of the discussion, whose interpretation alone trumps and norms all others. Nevertheless, those who bear his name or who profess to follow his doctrine presumably should be

16. Ibid., 170 (italics in original).
17. Ibid., 171.
18. Ibid., 189 (italics in original).

interested in understanding and following his course. Far too many interpreters of Luther have failed in this endeavor. In his contribution to a collection of essays on church and state, John Stumme also notes with dismay the equation of Luther's teaching with a sharp, American-style, separation of church and state that dominated Lutheran thinking during the first part of the twentieth century.[19] Stumme offers as his stellar example of the error the article "Church and State," written by Fredrick W. Stellhorn that appeared in "the important *The Lutheran Cyclopedia* of a century ago."[20] Stumme chose his example well. According to form, the article from the respected text relates a brief history of the interaction of church and state, including Lutheran state churches in Europe. "While he discredits the experience of Lutheran churches in Europe," Stumme observes, "Stellhorn enthusiastically endorses the form of church and state relations in the United States."[21] Stumme is not exaggerating. The article concludes with unabashed approval of the American way:

> Under the present circumstances, which will hardly ever change for the better, the total separation of Church and State, as in substance we have it in our United States is the only arrangement that is just and fair to all citizens. Its strict and perfect execution would, of course, do away with official prayer in Congress and Legislatures, with the reading of the Bible, or any religious book, in the public schools, and the like, and also render impossible any interference on the part of the State with the education of children demanded by the conscience of parents, as long as those children learn what the State has a right to demand its citizens should know. Luther entirely agreed with this principle of total separation between Church and State, but held that circumstances at his time were such that out of love to the Church the civil government had to take hold of the government of the Church also, and hoped the time would come when the correct principle could be carried out fully.[22]

Stellhorn, and most American Lutherans of his era, thought that hoped-for time had come at last. But as Stumme relates, such thinking

19. John R. Stumme, "A Lutheran Tradition on Church and State," in *Church and State: Lutheran Perspectives* (Minneapolis, MN: Fortress Press, 2003), 51–73.
20. Ibid., 52.
21. Ibid.
22. Henry Eyster Jacobs and John A. W. Haas, eds., *The Lutheran Cyclopedia* (New York: Charles Scribner's Sons, 1899), 108–9.

began to erode: "By mid-century voices arose that questioned the adequacy of separationism, which had become deeply entrenched in the piety of American Lutherans."[23] As will become abundantly clear, there is much evidence to support this claim of a growing dissatisfaction with the separationist position. On the contrary, there certainly were thinkers—perhaps those with an especially deeply entrenched piety—who kept holding fast and continued to endorse the total separation position articulated by Stellhorn in 1899. Some of those who maintained a position sympathetic to total separation have already been considered. Now, we turn to a roughly chronological sampling of those who criticized and targeted the "concept of total, complete, or absolute separation so eagerly embraced at the century's beginning."[24]

A New Way to Read Luther

Already in 1953, the *Lutheran Quarterly* featured a short but remarkable essay by George Forell, Herman Preus, and Jaroslav Pelikan, "Toward a Lutheran View of Church and State,"[25] which sought to shift thinking on the subject. A brief historical overview is provided, noting the advocacy of assorted versions of complete separation already by Tertullian, early monastic orders, the great German statesman, Bismarck, and of course, pious Lutherans: "Through the influence of Pietism, the theory of absolute separation made considerable impact upon Lutheranism."[26] The authors contend that many Lutherans of their day held that a Christian "should tolerate the state as a necessary evil, pay his taxes, and serve in the army, but otherwise should have as little as possible to do with the affairs of the state."[27] The authors correctly deem such thinking "a counsel of despair," and argue that it "ultimately surrenders too much of life to the powers of darkness."[28]

---

23. Stumme, "A Lutheran Tradition on Church and State," 53.
24. Ibid., 55.
25. George W. Forell, Herman A. Preus, and Jaroslav Pelikan, "Toward a Lutheran View of Church and State," *The Lutheran Quarterly* 5, no. 3 (Aug 1953): 280–90.
26. Ibid., 283.
27. Ibid.
28. Ibid., 284.

Especially troubling is the truth noted in the essay that "Such separation tends to give up the doctrine of creation, that God is Creator and Lord of both church and state and that his will is law in both realms."[29] This observation is exactly right, and a serious problem with any view that would support an absolute or complete separation of the realms. It is the church's failure to practice the full scope of its work that is the driving concern:

> Absolute separation of church and state denies the function of the Christian community to be the salt of the earth and the light shining in darkness. This assumes an interaction between the church and the state as well as the church and all other areas of life, for which the concept of absolute separation has not made adequate provision.[30]

Criticizing both state rule of the church and church rule of the state, the three theologians, instead, advocate an idea quite in keeping with Luther's own teaching and practice: "the interpenetration of church and state."[31] It is God who holds church and state together. "The fact that he is Lord of both," the essay states, "precludes absolute separation as well as the one-sided domination of the one over the other."[32] Each has its own task to fulfill, the state "primarily an agency of the Law (though it has an obligation to the Gospel)," and the church focused on the proclamation of the gospel "though it has an obligation to proclaim the Law" as well.[33] Of course, the church declares God's law in order to produce repentance, and thus, to open the door for the gospel's entry. "No one is exempt from the Law's accusation," the essay continues, "not even the king, and the church must be independent enough to speak the Law to the king for his repentance and the Gospel for his faith."[34] But this is not the only purpose of the law:

> The secondary function of the law is to uphold the order of the world, and when the church announces the Law it does so for this purpose too.

29. Ibid., 284–85.
30. Ibid., 285.
31. Ibid., 287.
32. Ibid.
33. Ibid., 288.
34. Ibid., 289.

The proclamation of the Word for the past twenty centuries has helped to sustain marriage and the home, and it has similarly been instrumental in teaching men the true nature of the state. . . . In a democracy the church has a peculiar opportunity to announce this Law to all who will hear, that citizens might recognize the true nature of the state and its relation to God.[35]

Without endorsing a confusion of the two realms, the authors promote a dynamic and lively interrelationship between God's two hands of activity in this world that should urge believers to a much more robust and serious engagement of the temporal realm.

Before leaving this seminal article, it is important to recognize that the authors maintain a firm grasp on the gospel without succumbing to either sentimentalism or some form of social gospel. The gospel is the forgiveness of sins in Christ and delivers eternal salvation. But it also has a profound impact on the way that Christians approach their lives in the temporal realm because it "teaches them to act within the situations into which God has called them, and to trust God for forgiveness."[36] Put more bluntly, the gospel gives believers the ability to enter into the messy realities of the present age, political and otherwise, without fear of eternal contamination or exclusion from God's grace. Forell, Preus, and Pelikan provide a compelling approach to the two realms that still resonates with relevance more than sixty years later. Their final appeal is worth hearing at length:

The life of the Gospel is a life of freedom and courage, of daring to work in the midst of the concrete world of parties and campaigns, caucuses and lobbies. As it proclaims the Word of God, the church warns men of the possibilities for sin operative in that world and at the same time reminds them of the possibilities for service operative there. In this way the church renders the state the highest possible service, producing men who are realistic without being cynical and principled without being quixotic.[37]

There is a simple appeal to this portrait, grounded, it can be argued, in the fact that these three theologians successfully maintain and

---

35. Ibid.
36. Ibid., 290.
37. Ibid.

advance the reality of the fertile tension that must always surge at the center of any faithful presentation of Luther's teaching.

Gerhard Ebeling

Less than a decade later, Gerhard Ebeling devoted an entire chapter of his book *Word and Faith* to "the necessity of the Doctrine of the Two Kingdoms."[38] The scholar's study of the topic is as rewarding as it is dense, closely relating the two kinds of righteousness with the two realms. This is hardly surprising, given that the author declares Luther's *Great Galatians Commentary* as a primary source. Of course, law and gospel also play a critical role as they did for the previous essay, but it is not a simple application: "much more careful differentiations will have to be made in relating the distinction between the two kingdoms to the distinction between law and Gospel."[39] Ebeling is definitely equal to the task. Unique among many who take up the topic, Ebeling is careful to expand the discussion of the two realms to include much more than just questions of church and state. To better appreciate Ebeling, a longer quote seems justified:

> Yet when we have acquired some familiarity with Luther's theological thinking, and take the trouble to view his statements not just statistically but reflectively, then it should be reasonably clear that under *regnum mundi* [the kingdom of the world] there falls the whole of reality *extra Christum* [outside of Christ], and that means *extra fidem* [beyond faith]—not merely its political aspect, but in the widest sense everything that concerns man, and thus everything that has to do with his *ratio* [reason], but also everything that has to do with his will and his passions, and hence absolutely everything from the most trifling human activity to science, morals and religion. Only in this broad sweep can the two kingdom doctrine be rightly interpreted.[40]

Ebeling is quite right both in his reading of Luther and in his counsel regarding the interpretation of the two realms.

Ebeling is also right, if somewhat less than lucid, when he calls

---

38. Gerhard Ebeling, *Word and Faith*, trans. James W. Leitch (London: SCM Press, 1963).
39. Ibid., 389.
40. Ibid., 393.

attention to the two very different ways that the two kingdoms can be understood, even in Luther. It is quite true that, at times, Luther uses the distinction for the "eschatological conflict between the divine and all that denies the divine, so that the victory of the one is the annihilation of the other."[41] Yet, at other times, the same terms are used to express the work of "preserving or restoring the relationship between Creator and creature, so that the vindication of the one is the glory of the other."[42] Reserving the term "two kingdoms" for the former and using "two orders" for the latter is Ebeling's suggested solution. The theologian admits that his suggestion is not grounded in Luther, but is not overly concerned: "This terminological separation, it is true, has no convincing basis in Luther's own way of speaking. Yet that would be no essential hindrance."[43] This awareness of Luther's different usages for the same vocabulary is essential for anyone seeking to arrive at a faithful understanding and application of the biblical doctrine.

It is, however, the intricate work of relating the two realms to the two kinds of righteousness, and then, exploring the reality of the two kinds of righteousness that is of particular interest to Ebeling, and occupies the latter part of the chapter. "Each of the two kingdoms," writes Ebeling, "has its *iustitia* [justice or righteousness]: the one has *iustitia civilis* [civil righteousness], and the other *iustitia Christiana* [Christian righteousness]."[44] His further work in distinguishing and relating these two kinds of righteousness, noting, for example, that "The two kinds of *iustitia* differ not in degree but qualitatively," is quite insightful and faithful to the work of the reformers.[45] Nevertheless, fascinating as it is, this path is tangential to the present task, and so, must be neglected for now. Still, a final observation made by Ebeling in relation to the two kinds of righteousness is worthy of mention as it also touches on the Christian's responsibility vis-à-vis the world:

41. Ibid., 397.
42. Ibid.
43. Ibid.
44. Ibid., 401.
45. Ibid.

For by works we can do justice only to the world, not to God. For that reason the criterion of works, precisely from the standpoint of the *iustitia civilis*, is love. In the realm of works there is no higher *iustitia* than the *iustitia civilis*! Yet for that very reason we should not imagine that with mere law-abidingness and bourgeois good conduct we have already done justice to the world and fulfilled all *iustitia civilis* in this basic sense.[46]

As a citizen of the world, a Christian is called to a life of works and service that can never be content with the world's verdict that he is "a good man." Rather, the Christian is under obligation to bring the full scope of God's justice to bear on the world that is encountered in the course of mundane life.

LCMS Efforts

Shortly after Ebeling's work appeared in English, Concordia Publishing House offered a contribution of their own to the conversation on church and state relationships with the publication of *Church and State under God*.[47] Written by an assembly of some of Missouri's noted theologians and scholars at mid-century, the text sought to cover multiple angles of the issue. For the purpose of this study, two of the chapters particularly stand out. Martin Scharlemann was entrusted with the book's opening chapter, an exemplary disquisition of biblical theology seeking to establish the scriptural grounding for the ensuing discussion. Even the editor notes Scharlemann's atypical course: "He does not simply bring together and interpret pertinent scripture passages. Rather, he evaluates the whole divine plan of human existence as revealed in the Word of God and describes the cosmic background which provides the setting for the functions of the church and of government."[48] This is a strength of the chapter and leads the author to produce a scholarly and discerning study, punctuated with some important observations and conclusions.

It is also true that the author displays a somewhat more pessimistic attitude toward the state per se than what was manifest in the two

46. Ibid., 405.
47. Albert G. Huegli, ed., *Church and State under God* (St. Louis, MO: Concordia, 1964).
48. Ibid., 13.

essays just considered. Acknowledging the debate over the origins of government, Scharlemann decides against those who would anchor it in the creation of man as a political being and asserts, "The state became necessary as a result of man's rebellion against God."[49] This line of thinking eventuates in the exegete making assertions that can be read as dismissive and even coining an expression later appropriated by Kurt Marquart. "In fact," writes Scharlemann, "governments exist mostly as a demonstration of God's patience with mankind while His people are being gathered from the four corners of the earth. The state is part of the scaffolding for the kingdom of heaven."[50] As mentioned above, this is hardly the most felicitous choice of images and seems to abet an attitude that judges the material world as unworthy of the serious attention of God or God's people. Scharlemann's position is consistent, however, and the scaffolding imagery fits with his view of the role of government. "The church and its members on their part have the responsibility of honoring and respecting government for what God intends it to be: a bulwark against anarchy."[51] For Scharlemann, the state's purpose is, at best, wholly negative. With such a constrained understanding of the task of government, the role of the Christian with regard to the state is quite simple: "With this statement we come to the chief responsibility of the Christian: to be subject."[52] This thought leads the professor to reflect further on the significance of a spirit of submission and yields one of the bright moments of the essay in the form of a potent apothegm. "In their attitude of self-effacement," Scharlemann observes, "Christians live out the strange paradox that man can gain inner freedom only by subjecting himself to that which is above him."[53] This very Pauline notion deserves further consideration, but would certainly lead to a rather serious detour from the present discussion.[54]

---

49. Ibid., 24.
50. Ibid., 53.
51. Ibid., 50.
52. Ibid., 51.
53. Ibid.
54. The topic of freedom's true nature is elaborated and advanced on these lines in an important essay by Reinhard Hütter. See his "(Re-)Forming Freedom: Reflections 'after *Veritatis Splendor*' on

While Scharlemann writes an essay that seems to exhibit the familiar attitude of suspicion, condescension, or mere tolerance toward the temporal realm that was demonstrated by the authors first considered in this chapter, he makes several key points about the interrelationship between church and state, which set him apart and advance the argument. Writing in the throes of the Cold War, Scharlemann wonders about the extent of the church's responsibility toward the government in a totalitarian state. "In a free way of society, on the other hand," he counters, "the church and the individual Christian have maximum responsibilities also for the social order."[55] As Scharlemann proceeds to define the content of these responsibilities, he sounds a different tone than mere endurance of the temporal realm. Especially in a democracy, in order to shoulder his responsibility for government, the individual Christian "must help to shape the content and direction of public opinion."[56] Scharlemann makes this point even more strongly: "The Christian citizen has as great an obligation as anyone—in fact a great deal more than others—to get out into the marketplace [of ideas] to articulate his own convictions and beliefs so that government may indeed stay on course or return to its proper sphere."[57] Citing their solid grasp of the source of political authority, the author even calls on Christians "to seek public office wherever possible and necessary."[58] Finally, but not insignificantly, individual Christians serve the temporal realm by praying for it.

With individual Christians, the corporate body of the church in its divine service also uses prayer as a primary means of serving the state and the wider society. But this intercessory prayer is not insipid or timid and should never become a prop for the state or a blind affirmation of government. Scharlemann is insistent:

> Of course, such prayers should not be so worded as to suggest that the church underwrites every action of government, for the church must

Freedom's Fate in Modernity and Protestantism's Antinomian Captivity," *Modern Theology* 17, no. 2 (April 2001): 117–61.

55. Ibid., 55.
56. Ibid.
57. Ibid., 55–56.
58. Ibid. 56.

always stand above civic administration and apart from injustice. Above all else the church must refuse to let itself be made the instrument of any political movement that may assume a messianic character. . . . At times it must even take its position with Ambrose of old in his condemnation of both emperor and empress for the wrongs they had done.[59]

The church is called upon to confront unrighteousness even in the highest levels of government. But it is not only the government that is the concern of the corporate church; it also has a responsibility to teach the wider culture about God's law. Again, Scharlemann is forceful in his assertion: "We cannot possibly stress too strongly that the church also teaches the Law as a curb on unrighteousness. It must be vitally interested, therefore, in what our Confessions call civic righteousness. It is not true to its full task if it fails to support and insist on this quality of life in society at large."[60] This is a bold declaration, representing a significant departure from any notion of absolute separation that endorses a "live and let live" mindset. The church must engage with the wider culture, "it cannot therefore ignore or remain indifferent to groups and forces that encourage upright living."[61] Beyond the task of teaching God's law to society, the church also needs to be intentional about sharpening the consciences of individual members and guarding "the essential distinction between the church and the state."[62]

Scharlemann closes his chapter with one last plea that speaks to the present day perhaps even more pointedly than it did to the world of 1964:

To that end the church will lend all its energies to the task of keeping states from being purely secular institutions in the sense that they ignore the existence of God. And the church will most certainly never grow weary in the task of preventing government from becoming demonic, that is, displacing God by its own claims on the total life of man.[63]

59. Ibid., 57.
60. Ibid., 58.
61. Ibid.
62. Ibid.
63. Ibid.

The referents that filled Scharlemann's mind as he wrote these words may have been on the other side of a curtain of iron or bamboo. Five decades later, that menace has diminished if not disappeared; but it may well be that the threat of the demonic as defined by Scharlemann has mushroomed and now lies much nearer at hand.

Lewis Spitz

Immediately following Scharlemann's exegetical grounding of the discussion, the editor of *Church and State under God* predictably placed an essay on the historical background of the discussion. Also, somewhat predictably, considering the unabashedly Lutheran character of the text, the history that is of interest is Reformation history. Lewis Spitz was more than equal to the task and provided a careful and convincing synopsis of the significance of the Reformation on issues of church and state. While Spitz's historical account of Luther's relevant writings and practice is worthwhile in its own right, for the purposes of this chapter, what is of particular interest is the fact that the author articulates Luther's distinctive thinking with exacting clarity and without any attempt to chide or temper the reformer for what some, such as Pieper, saw as Luther's incautious or inconsistent practice. Any alert and competent contemporary reader of Spitz's essay is forcefully confronted with ideas on church and state that do not readily square with the complete separation ideas advanced by earlier—and later—twentieth-century Lutheran scholars.

Frequently in the essay, Spitz calls attention to Luther's rather active involvement in the political world of his own day. Describing Luther's characteristic concrete handling of social issues including questions of church and state, Spitz provides a helpful summary of Luther's stance:

> He was passionately political in his concern for the welfare of the people and the prospering of the cause, but he left behind no treatise on statecraft or commentary on the medieval-Aristotelian ideals of civic life. His own last journey was undertaken through icy storms in the dead of winter to restore amity between two territorial princes, the counts of Mansfeld, who were brothers. His final sermons outspokenly criticize the vices of rulers and the necessity for their obedience to the laws of God.[64]

Spitz recognizes that Luther's willingness to engage and serve the temporal realm was in full harmony with his "new ethos of Christian vocation" that allowed the old dualism between sacred and secular to be overcome, and the secular realm to be ennobled and rightly valued.[65] "God's majesty," Spitz writes, "was revealed in the created world, to which government as a divine ordinance also belonged."[66] Nothing suspicious or sinister inherently attached to temporal authority. Rather, Spitz points out that Luther and the other reformers "enlarged the state's area of competence—in charities and education, for example."[67] Indeed, Spitz continues, "Luther, who had a lively interest in social life and the order of the state, Zwingli, Calvin, and many Anglicans were political activists."[68] Taken together, Spitz limns a portrait of Luther and the resultant Lutheran thinking on two realms that bears little resemblance to the detached, distrustful, and disdainful attitude that would look askance at everything outside the church as mere scaffolding for what truly matters.

Luther's firm grasp on the revolutionary teaching of vocation certainly provided solid support for his positive assessment of the temporal realm and its rulers. But, another factor, also noted by Spitz, is the even more foundational idea that government is merely one aspect of the much broader arena of the material or created world. Spitz observes that this thinking is firmly expressed also in the Confessions: "In the Symbols government is part of a larger sphere of external activity which includes man's total corporeal, political, economic, and social life."[69] All of this wide, sweeping reality was of interest to God; indeed, it was his creation, and his work in Christ was aimed at its restoration. "In the regime of the state," Spitz tells us, Luther believed that "the immanent God is at work in the natural order, also through men, establishing peace and prosperity on earth."[70]

---

64. Ibid., 63.
65. Ibid., 109.
66. Ibid.
67. Ibid.
68. Ibid.
69. Ibid., 91.
70. Ibid., 63.

The presence of God's ordering and directing will in the form of natural law, God's "unwritten law whose requirements lay imbedded in reality itself," further proved the extent of God's provision for the material world and the temporal rulers directly charged with its care.[71] Spitz goes on to provide a splendid but, for my purposes, also tangential digest of Lutheran thinking about natural law. A final point that illustrates Spitz's departure from more dichotomizing or separatist Lutheran views of church and state appears when he discusses Luther's willingness to admonish princes when necessary. Of course, as all theologians confidently assert, Christians are "conscience-bound to disobey" a prince who "tyrannically interferes in matters of faith."[72] But, quoting and then following Luther, Spitz goes further:

> "You should not approve of your adversary's sin but warn and rebuke him. . . . For thus you save your conscience," Luther admonished. Whoever remains silent makes himself an accomplice. Ministers bear a special responsibility as public spokesmen in the Christian assembly. "There are lazy and useless preachers who do not denounce the evils of the princes and lords, some because they do not even notice them. . . . Some even fear for their skins and worry that they will lose body and goods for it. They do not stand up and be true to Christ."[73]

Spitz puts an exclamation point on the nature and extent of Luther's admonition with a sentence of three words that are likely to provoke chills and a cold sweat in many readers of his day and ours: "He named names."[74] In the course of simply reporting on the "Impact of the Reformation on Church-State Issues," Spitz manages to present an understanding of the interface of the two realms that is vital, dynamic, and hardly supportive of a strict and neat separationism.

Heinrich Bornkamm

Unquestionably shaped by his experiences in Germany of the 1930s and later, Luther scholar Heinrich Bornkamm offered a brief volume

71. Ibid., 76.
72. Iibd., 70.
73. Ibid.
74. Ibid.

devoted to a discussion of Luther's teaching on the two realms. The English translation appeared in 1966. Bornkamm's thorough understanding of Luther is evident as he explicates the reformer's teaching outlined in "Temporal Authority." The essay totals less than forty pages, yet proves remarkably rewarding. What follows can do little more than sample some of the particularly relevant points in the presentation. The author supplies a clear overview of Luther's conception of the twofold rule of God, and stresses the bond that must unite them:

> Luther distinguishes the respective "kingdoms" or "governments" in a meaningful but not pedantic way. For they belong together inseparably. Luther always had to assert two things: (a) that there are for the Christian two real and clearly separated sets of life-relationships; but (b) that these "kingdoms" are not rigidly fixed provinces into which the Christian's existence is divided.[75]

The Christian must work actively and continually to discern what is expected of him at any given moment. As Bornkamm writes, "he is to use the means of the one or the other 'government' in order to carry out the will of God, which holds the world together."[76] Bornkamm's emphasis on the unity of the two kingdoms is further sharpened when he locates the unity not only in the one will of God, but in the individual Christian person: "Overarching the deep abyss which the Middle Ages had sought to bridge by means of a church controlling both spiritual and secular power, Luther discovered a completely different form of unity—the unity of the Christian person as obligated in both sets of relationships."[77] God's realms come together in the individual Christian who lives in both simultaneously.

Bornkamm is convinced that it is the Christian's existence in the world that drives Luther's teaching of the two realms. In particular, the author contends that for Luther, it was the difficulty of reconciling the radical demands of the Sermon on the Mount with the realities of

---

75. Heinrich Bornkamm, *Luther's Doctrine of the Two Kingdoms: In the Context of His Theology* (Philadelphia, PA: Fortress Press, 1966), 8.
76. Ibid., 9.
77. Ibid., 26.

life in the temporal realm that became "the decisive impetus for the reformulation of the two kingdoms doctrine."[78] This means that the doctrine is far from ethereal or distantly intellectual. It springs from the concrete challenges that inevitably arise when a Christian strives to live the confession of Christ. "The doctrine of the two kingdoms," Bornkamm argues, "is nothing other than a description of the Christian's situation in the world."[79] As a child of God, the Christian lives only and always for the sake of the gospel and follows his Lord on a self-denying, all-consuming course of sacrificial giving fully in the spirit of the Sermon on the Mount. As a creature bound to the material world, the Christian at the same time lives in the complexity and danger of a broken world where the sword is mandated and rightly wielded for the sake of others. These seemingly disparate truths are inseparably fused in the believer:

> Everything depends on grasping that we are not dealing with a tearing asunder of the world into two rigidly separated realms, but with a question of perspectives; it is one and the same world, but seen from two different viewpoints, "for me—for others," which the Christian must always choose between in making fresh and living decisions.[80]

The fact of the Christian's twofold yet singular existence is, in Bornkamm's view, one of three dimensions of the teaching of the two kingdoms. The other two are "the relationship between church and state" and "the relationship, in general, between the spiritual and the secular, the kingdom of Christ and the kingdom of the world."[81] This threefold distinction, especially the second dimension, is Bornkamm's effort to account for Luther's oft-noted fluid use of terminology. "But these three dimensions," Bornkamm continues, "are only aspects of one and the same problem: that of the basic relationship between the gospel and the order of this world."[82]

---

78. Ibid., 23.
79. Ibid., 13.
80. Ibid., 14.
81. Ibid., 16.
82. Ibid.

Precisely at this juncture in the argument, Bornkamm supplies one of many significant observations about the two realms:

> Only in the relation between church and state is there a discernible boundary between their respective offices and duties; there is no such boundary in the relation of the Christian to life in the world. The line of demarcation in his activity is drawn no less sharply, but it is hidden, and must be sought in repeated decisions of conscience. The mistaken transfer to the Christian life of the model of church and state as clearly distinguished realms has often given the impression of a dualistic sundering of life.[83]

The Christian's task of determining when to act for self or for others, whether to turn the other cheek or to raise the sword in justice is rarely easily managed. While seeking to negotiate the murky interface between these two obligations, the Christian is distinguishing between what is done as a private person—the path of self-denial—and what is done as a public person—the route taken with sword in hand. This tension grips all. None are exempt: "But all of us," Bornkamm declares, "are *publicae personae* [public persons], office-holders, insofar as we participate in the life of the community. We must therefore share in this constant vigilance lest the order of justice be destroyed and the world be surrendered to brute force."[84] It seems beyond dispute that this obligation as a public person is only magnified in the context of a representative democracy. The Christian's duty is clear; the specific path to be followed in any given situation, however, is often far from clear. Signaling the importance of this point, in the essay's final paragraph, Bornkamm returns again to the believer's sacred responsibility for the world:

> Only if one misunderstands the two kingdom doctrine in a Manichean, dualistic sense can one think oneself free, as a Christian, to leave the world to its own devices—exactly the opposite of what Luther intended. The two kingdom doctrine is not a social-ethical program, neither one to be left behind nor one to be retained. It is the indispensable means of orientation which the Christian must again and again employ when considering his

83. Ibid., 17.
84. Ibid., 23.

role and action in the world. It makes it possible for him to live according to the command of Jesus in the midst of the orders of this existence, orders marked by signs of the end and yet still preserved by God.[85]

A more eloquent or accurate appeal to faithful Christian activism seems unlikely.

Paul Althaus

Another German who directly confronted both the significance and the complexities of rightly distinguishing the two realms was Paul Althaus. In concert with the theologians already considered, Althaus presents his own thinking in the context of explicating Luther's teaching. Like Bornkamm, he has high regard for the reformer's contribution to rightly understanding and navigating the Christian's interface with the temporal realm. He makes no effort to soft pedal or obscure Luther's twofold distinction, stating bluntly, "Luther's doctrine of the two kingdoms is one of the most valuable and enduring treasures of his theology."[86] Considering a general attitude of opprobrium widely attached to Luther's teaching of the two realms during the Cold War years, this assertion of Althaus is all the more remarkable. In a tangential way, he addresses the popular but misguided conviction that identified Luther's teaching as a precipitating factor in the horror that was the Third Reich:

> Luther never abandons the political world to autonomous self-administration; rather, he constantly struggles against the self-glorification of the princes and their misuse of the secular government. He clearly admonishes the consciences of politicians to conform to the will of God. The emancipation of political governments from any moral concern does not have its source in Martin Luther but in the Renaissance.[87]

Of course, Althaus is aware that errant teaching may have claimed the seal of Lutheran authenticity, when in fact, it was nothing of the

---

85. Ibid., 37.
86. Paul Althaus, *The Ethics of Martin Luther*, trans. Robert C. Schulz (Minneapolis, MN: Fortress Press, 1972), 82.
87. Ibid.

sort: "Later misuse of this teaching to set government and politics free from the norms of morality is not based on Luther's doctrine itself, and we cannot hold Luther responsible for it."[88] Althaus emphasizes repeatedly that Luther's own actions belied the notion that the reformer somehow spawned quietism and servile compliance as he regularly held princes accountable to God's moral law.

Indeed, Althaus notes that Luther was not content with providing moral correctives or general encouragement to his princes. It was not enough that they observe the level of general morality expected of all people. Additionally, princes must use their office and their reason to accomplish God's purpose of preserving life. "Luther constantly reasserted this," Althaus observes, "not only in general statements but also by making very specific criticisms and by giving directions for specific activities."[89] In the context of their vocations as temporal rulers, Luther was willing to enter the fray with and against princes, and believed that all clergy shouldered this same responsibility toward rulers:

> Luther felt that the clergy also had the duty to admonish the princes seriously and urge them to wage war whenever they were lazy and did not decisively fulfill their duty to defend their subjects with the sword when they were attacked. Luther himself did exactly this both in the Peasant's War and when the Turks were threatening attack.[90]

A pastor could do this work since "the political office and the preaching office of the ministry encounter each other at the point of God's law."[91] Althaus's recognition of the common ground of God's law is significant because it moves the church's use of the law beyond merely its convicting or crushing work and into the norming or guiding aspect: "The preaching of the law has been committed to the church not merely insofar as, understood in its depth, it reveals the sin of men and leads them toward the gospel but also insofar as it is intended to preserve order in the world."[92] The church and her pastor are under

88. Ibid., 81.
89. Ibid., 80.
90. Ibid., 139.
91. Ibid., 148.

Job of Pastor in the secular realm

obligation not just to deliver spiritual truth and goods, but also to insure the right functioning of the temporal realm—that is, according to the will of God.

Aware of the charge that following Luther and thinking in terms of two distinct realms with very different goals and means cannot avoid devolving into a de facto Christian schizophrenia, Althaus contends, "On the contrary, a deep and basic unity prevails in the midst of the difference and opposition."[93] This unity is founded in the reality that whatever the Christian does, whether as an individual person or as one who holds an office in the temporal realm, it is done in humility at the command of God and in service to others. "The only difference," Althaus observes, "is that in one case service occurs in direct personal encounters between people and in the other case through the structures and orders which support the life of society and through which the Christian serves his brothers."[94] So, the same Christian may "turn the other cheek," and refuse to dispute a neighbor's manufactured and false legal claim to a parcel of land rightly owned by the Christian; and then, in the course of discharging the duties of the office of District Attorney, prosecute that same neighbor for animal abuse. Althaus is confident that Luther's understanding is quite right. "In all this," he asserts, "Luther stands much closer to Jesus and the New Testament than did Tolstoi [sic], who felt that service in government could not be reconciled with being a disciple of Jesus."[95] Of course, Althaus recognizes that this twofold nature of the Christian life creates a tension that "is great indeed," as there is often a collision between "our personal attitude and our objective activity for the sake of justice, between love in our hearts and the severity of our administration of justice."[96] Nevertheless, this tension is cause for neither surprise nor alarm as "the same deep tension is found in God himself."[97] God is love, yet delivers justice as necessary. God employs

92. Ibid.
93. Ibid., 70.
94. Ibid., 70–71.
95. Ibid., 71.
96. Ibid., 77.
97. Ibid.

brute force against those who rebel against him even as he loves them. "God's love appears in our evil world also in the broken form of his wrath—as his 'strange work.'"[98] There is, then, a correspondence between the ethical paradox of a Christian humbly loving yet meting out justice and the theological paradox of God's activity. For Althaus, this is quite significant because it means that Luther's "solution of the problem of the Christian in political office is not based on a compromise."[99] It is the nature of God and God's work in the world that grounds Luther's teaching.

Finally, Althaus briefly addresses an issue that will command greater attention when the question of the continuing relevance and significance of Luther's two realms teaching is considered more fully in the next chapter. The Luther scholar freely concedes the historical grounding and influence evident in the specific applications Luther makes of his own doctrine. But while Althaus recognizes the enormous differences between Luther's world and the present situation in the Western world, he insists on the abiding importance of Luther's teaching. He writes, "Our world is different from the world in which Luther lived. And Luther's ideas must be reinterpreted and applied in terms of this new situation. However, their basic structure continues to demonstrate its truth."[100] Considering the seemingly innate human propensity for each generation to privilege its own moment and to rank contemporary problems, challenges, and needs as singular and without precedent, Althaus's insistence on the enduring truth and relevance of Luther's teaching deserves to be heard and heeded.

Ulrich Duchrow

A generation or so after Althaus, Ulrich Duchrow would write and publish widely from his post as professor of systematic theology at the University of Heidelberg, often attacking what he saw as the dangers and injustices implicit in the capitalism of Western society. Early in his

---

98. Ibid.
99. Ibid.
100. Ibid., 82.

career, however, he edited *Lutheran Churches—Salt or Mirror of Society?*
and wrote introductory and concluding essays for the book, which
are not manifestos for a particular agenda but are theoretical and
foundational in nature, and so, of interest here.[101] It is important in this
regard, indeed as it is with the bulk of the authors considered in this
chapter, to distinguish between a theoretical or theological foundation
and the structure that is built upon it. It is entirely possible that a
thinker can do one well, and flounder in the work of the other—though
the possibility of succeeding at the second while failing at the first
is remote indeed. Duchrow seeks to explicate Luther's teaching and
recognizes a simple truth at the center of that teaching: all human
institutions, including ecclesial, political, and economic, serve "God's
loving will" which "is to combat the powers of evil," and in this task,
these institutions "serve one another." As a result, Duchrow continues,
"This means that God's twofold governance (spiritual and temporal)
and the human institutions employed for this task are, in Luther's
opinion, neither dualistically opposed to each other nor inter-
dependent, but complementary and interrelated."[102] The church, then,
and not just the individual Christian is bound to the temporal realm
and obligated to serve it. More specifically, Duchrow contends, "this
meant not abjuring the status quo, as is often maintained, but rather
it meant that Christians and the church should actively participate in
the struggle to improve economic, social and public institutions—even
at the risk of enduring persecution and the cross."[103] The objectives
of this struggle are not as vague as it might seem: "The crucial test
in determining whether the institutions are concerned about
safeguarding the common good is this: do they protect and care for
the well-being of the weakest member of society?"[104] Clearly, different
readers may have different thoughts about who best qualifies as the

---

101. Ulrich Duchrow, ed., *Lutheran Churches—Salt or Mirror of Society?: Case Studies on the Theory and Practice of the Two Kingdoms Doctrine* (Geneva: Lutheran World Federation, 1977).
102. Ibid., 4.
103. Ibid., 9.
104. Ibid., 296.

66

weakest members of society, yet the principle seems altogether consistent with scripture and with Luther.

Duchrow is quite aware of the very real possibility that Luther's teaching can be wrongly understood and disastrously applied. He acknowledges the threat posed by those who advocate "one governance," with either state or church swallowing the other, but his Lutheran context makes him more concerned about errors of hyper-dualism.[105] When the two realms are pushed into exclusive and completely separate spheres, they end up functioning with what Duchrow considers an erroneous autonomy. Depicting and criticizing this line of thinking, Duchrow writes:

> The church is expected to remain politically neutral, to transcend the political parties. It is regarded as having the right to speak out on principles but not on concrete situations. Of course, the church does speak out whenever its own economic or ideological interests as an institution are affected, or whenever the interests of the majority of the church's membership permit or require it to speak out. In this respect, it may even come to pass that concrete criticism in political affairs is tolerated in a few instances, as long as the church's vital institutional interests or those of the power groups in the existing social system are not affected.[106]

In the context of contemporary America, it is certainly no great challenge to find tangible examples to match Duchrow's description; exactly this conception of the two kingdoms is prevalent. Inevitably, such a false application of the dialectic also pushes the church into a spiritual or domestic corner. "The essential meaning of religion and of the church," writes Duchrow, "could find expression only in the realm of private life, and even then only in personal relationships and within the family. The economic, scientific, and public spheres of life were expected to be accepted and sanctioned automatically."[107] Efforts to confine the place and work of the church so narrowly are not remarkable—that such efforts originate in the church is remarkable, or it should be.

---

105. Ibid., 301–3.
106. Ibid., 303.
107. Ibid., 15.

Instead of complicity with the state and blind affirmation, or disavowal of the state and disgusted rejection—both of which can result from pushing Luther's two realms teaching into a radical dualism—Duchrow calls the church to a more scriptural and Lutheran role. "Not conformity to the existing powers," he argues, "but critical examination to discover what is God's good will for humankind, is the path of the Christian church."[108] Naturally, this is more easily stated than accomplished. Human sin and the quest for comfort can also corrupt those in the church and tempt them to follow the reliably pleasant path of inoffensive and harmless quietism. Nevertheless, a right understanding of Luther's teaching offers no space for quietism or simple separation of the realms. Rather, the church, and specifically, the office of the ministry "must 'instruct' all the '*Stände*' (estates) on how to conduct themselves in the sight of God in their social and political activities." Indeed, "Ministry ought to devote special attention to those who wield power, to show them what is true and right."[109] In the process of discharging this duty with diligence, the church will certainly be compelled to make distinctions among different ideas and policies and even individuals. Duchrow understands and supports this:

> The assumption that is so popular today—that the church must retain its ideological neutrality is, first of all, a helpless self-deception, and secondly, un-Lutheran and unbiblical, because the Holy Spirit is bestowed expressly to enable us to discern God's will in every concrete situation (to cite Romans 12:1-2 once more!).[110]

For the church to speak faithfully, boldly, and effectively to and about the temporal realm, it must be freed from constraint, it must be free from reliance on the state. "If the church really wants to cooperate with God against the powers of evil and to serve the whole human being in his total relationship with others and in his total 'secular' life, then it must enjoy the greatest possible independence from the powers of this world."[111] Duchrow is right, but his sharp point mightily disturbs

108. Ibid., 299.
109. Ibid., 312.
110. Ibid., 316.
111. Ibid., 309.

not only the tidy arrangements of European state churches, but also demands an honest and piercing reassessment of the price paid for the American church's precious "tax-exempt" status. Such potentially unsettling thoughts deserve more attention, and will receive it in chapter 5.

Late Modern American Lutheranism

My intent here is to provide overwhelming evidence that an accurate reading and appropriation of Luther's teaching on the two realms does not culminate in a radical separation of the two realms, any sort of disparagement of the temporal realm, or a prescribed quietism that excuses and fortifies the church's absence from the temporal realm. Rather, read and understood rightly, Luther provides an exceptional tool to guide both the individual Christian and the church as a whole rightly to regard and engage with the temporal realm and its obligations. The theologians already considered—beginning with Pelikan, Preus, and Forell—emphasize different aspects and nuances of Luther's teaching, but none offers support to any thoughts of complete separation, quietism, or autonomous spheres. And there are more who do the same, many more.

Richard John Neuhaus, when still within the Lutheran fold, and actually with great consistency until his death, offered an understanding of the interface of church and world that was wholly compatible with Luther's teaching. Ever cautious of the church compromising its voice by too eagerly and too often inserting itself into the temporal realm—especially policy questions of the temporal realm—he was also an unashamed proponent of democracy, did not contemptuously dismiss capitalism, and viewed America's role and influence in the world charitably.[112] His guidance on the appropriate extent of the church's direct engagement with government policy is a bon mot worthy of memorization: "When it is not necessary for the church to speak, it is necessary for the church not to speak."[113] But, this

---

112. Richard John Neuhaus, *American Babylon: Notes of a Christian Exile* (Philadelphia, PA: Basic Books, 2010).

did not mean that the church should retire from public life. In fact, as he argued persuasively in the much referenced *The Naked Public Square*, the church had a vital role to play in the temporal realm, for the sake of the temporal realm.[114] For Neuhaus, the temporal realm, including the government of that realm, was worthy of the church's attention and effort—but not in the way that many inside and outside the church assumed.

Another theologian and political thinker who, like Neuhaus, grasped the responsibility of the church toward government, and yet, expressed no great love for typical left-of-center activist agendas, is Robert Benne. His *The Paradoxical Vision* offers a thoroughgoing presentation of a right understanding and practice of Luther's thinking on the two realms. Benne's penetrating taxonomy of four pyramiding levels of ecclesial interface with the culture—from the broad base of unintentional and indirect, to the pinnacle of direct use of power and influence—has proven exceedingly useful.[115] The same text provides another serviceable gift with the image of the church's teaching and degree of commitment to each broad category of teaching as a series of concentric rings. Benne's dynamic image provides exceptional guidance in teaching the church how to approach and answer the questions encountered when the church strives to heed God's command in the temporal realm.

Journalist and adept cultural observer Uwe Siemon-Netto not only provided a voice that can be enlisted in the harmonic chorus assembled here with his rejection of radical separationism as well as the quietism wrongly attributed to Luther, but he went further and offered specific historical examples of German Lutherans rightly and actively practicing the teaching of Luther and confronting temporal rulers both during World War II and at the close of the Cold War.[116] His research

---

113. Quoted in *Render unto Caesar . . . and unto God: A Lutheran View of Church and State*, St. Louis: A Report of the Commission on Theology and Church Relations of the Lutheran Church—Missouri Synod. September, 1995, 65.

114. Richard John Neuhaus, *The Naked Public Square: Religion and Democracy in America* (Grand Rapids, MI: Eerdmans, 1984).

115. Robert Benne, *The Paradoxical Vision: A Public Theology for the Twenty-First Century* (Minneapolis, MN: Fortress Press, 1995), 184–224. A CTCR document produced by the LCMS made extensive use of this taxonomy. C.f. *Render unto Caesar . . . and unto God* September, 1995, 67–90.

confirms the position of Neuhaus and Benne—that a right understanding of Luther's teaching can never be bent to condone quietism, yet neither must it eventuate in ardent advocacy for standard Enlightenment-bred liberal cultural and societal standards and ambitions. Finally, one more contemporary voice will serve to complete this chapter's catalog of witnesses. Craig Nessan, professor at Wartburg Seminary, has suggested that using the word "strategies" rather than "kingdoms" helps to reinforce the idea that "Luther's two kingdoms teaching is not about two separate and unrelated *realms,* but rather about two different types of divine *activity.*"[117] This is certainly a right emphasis, and the shift in words helps to illustrate the dynamic nature of the paradigm, though it is not clear why *strategies* is any less inherently dichotomous than *kingdoms* or *realms.* Regardless of the terminology, Nessan's goal is right: that Christians would do God's will "by living responsibly not only by testifying to the Gospel of Jesus Christ but at the same time by active political engagement."[118] The direction and form of that active political engagement can be wide and varied, of course, but Nessan is quite right to expect it.

A Legacy Neglected

Surrounded by an assembly of theologians, all advocating a far more vigorous and kinetic intersection and interaction between God's two realms, the question unavoidably asserts itself again: Why do not more North American Christians, and especially Lutherans, recognize and practice what has been so clearly taught? I remain persuaded that a complete explanation is better sought and offered by those qualified, or at least at liberty, for such pursuits; but I suspect that the answer has more than a little to do with the inescapable consequences of living long in the United States. Whatever the founding fathers may or may not have intended, the American public now takes for granted

116. Uwe Siemon-Netto, *The Fabricated Luther: The Rise and Fall of the Shirer Myth* (St. Louis, MO: Concordia, 1995).

117. Craig L. Nessan, "Lutheran Social Ministry: Reclaiming Luther's Kingdoms," *Misso Apostolica* 11, no. 2 (Nov 2003): 93 (emphasis in original).

118. Craig L. Nessan, "Reappropriating Luther's Two Kingdoms," *Lutheran Quarterly* 19 (2005): 309–10.

that the separation of church and state is an American ideal; and for most, this means very simply that religion and politics are—aside from sentimental and inconsequential bits of tradition like crèches and crosses on public land, and prayers before public events—incompatible and mutually exclusive.[119] Ever eager to prove their civic righteousness, many American Christians, especially Lutheran ones, it seems, have readily adopted the separation dictum recognizing it, in their estimation, to be wise, enlightened, and vaguely spiritual. Thus, Luther's actual teaching about the relationship of Christians as well as the church with the wider world is forfeited for a simplistic and wrong view, with roots not in scripture or Reformation doctrine, but in Enlightenment political theory. Plainly, the solution is not another book or essay—the many already available have yet to make any appreciable impact. Books left unread, and truths not taught are essentially nonexistent. Teaching, then, needs to shift, and the revision must permeate all levels from home to parish to seminary. Luther's legacy is ready at hand; his heirs must be taught to hear him rightly, and then, to act on that teaching with courage. The principal beneficiary of such a change would not be the Christian or even the church, but the world, God's world. Indeed, the world urgently needs Luther's understanding of the two realms taught accurately and ardently. The resources are waiting. The teaching must begin.

119. It is worth remembering that the Constitution of the United States does not contain the language of separation of church and state, and there is hardly clarity or universal agreement on what exactly is meant by the First Amendment's non-establishment clause.

3

Two Realms for Today: Suitable and Wholly Relevant

As much as Luther is praised from widely divergent and disparate quarters for his progressive and often revolutionary ideas about an assortment of issues, ranging from educating and rearing children, to advice for domesticate tranquility, to the importance of the individual person within the societal structure, to overturning unjust lending practices, he is as often—and not atypically by the same people—criticized and dismissed as hopelessly enslaved to a medieval, and so, it is assumed irrelevant and largely worthless, worldview when it comes to other issues, especially those involving women, rulers, authority, and religion. Of course, the line between what is lauded and what is rejected in the work of the reformer does have to be drawn somewhere, and every reader and interpreter of Luther draws one.

Drawing the Line

Naturally, the place that one draws the line is largely, if not entirely, dependent on the presuppositions at work before beginning the evaluation. Those enmeshed in a thoroughgoing enchantment with an enlightened and empirical worldview may appreciate the reformer's advocacy for gentle discipline, the enlightened foresight of including girls alongside boys in his calls for educating the youth, and his spirited stand against pope and emperor; meanwhile, all matters touching on "metaphysics" or theology per se (in other words, the overwhelming majority of the reformer's work) are deemed irrelevant nonsense and consigned to a place on the far side of their what-is-acceptable-line. Some theologians will applaud Luther's "reforming spirit," eagerly emulate him with a similar posture in their own activities, but then, criticize and reject the actual content of Luther's "dated" and "overly dogmatic" doctrinal positions. Still, the truth is that not even the most sympathetic and conservative reader of Luther can avoid drawing a line that excludes at least some of the former monk's views. One would be hard-pressed to find twenty-first-century people willing to endorse Luther unreservedly on the reasons and the remedies he suggests for his numerous bodily ailments, or his penchant for suggesting fascinating but often unsubstantiated etymologies of words. Some of Luther must always be left behind in his peculiar sixteenth-century, idiosyncratic world.

The pressing question for this book is whether or not one can safely draw the line of what is acceptable in Luther broadly and generously enough to include the Wittenberger's teaching on the two realms. In other words, does Luther's genius extend beyond theological method and doctrinal formulation to include also his understanding of the dynamic, yet precise and deliberate, distinction between the spiritual and the temporal realms; or, is Luther's thinking in this area simply one of those pieces of medieval baggage or individual eccentricities best left in the archives of history or quarantined to the field of personality study? To put an even finer point on the question, it can be asked this way: Does Luther's extensive counsel on the right relation between the church and the state, between God's ministers of the Word and the servants of the sword, apply with equal force in every time and in every place, or should it be sharply restricted and applied only to a world of robust Constantinianism like his own, or at the very least, to a Western "Christianized" setting?

The answer to this question is obviously of vital importance to the work of this book. As one would expect, opinions on this score are far from unanimous. To this point, this study has considered only scholars and thinkers who take for granted the suitability of Luther's teaching for their own world. While the disparate collection of theologians considered in the previous chapter interpreted Luther's teaching of the two realms in a variety of sometimes conflicting ways, they were alike—with no indication of misgivings or necessary caveats—in taking for granted the applicability and relevance of Luther's teaching for the contemporary political situation that surrounded them. But not all have seen it this way, and before proceeding with my own work of applying Luther's teaching to the church's contemporary situation, it is necessary to consider the possibility that Luther's relevance for today's socio/political questions is moot or negated altogether. Of course, disparaging the reformer's teaching and practice requires no actual knowledge of either. A critique that deserves a hearing, then, must emanate from a credible source. A representative pair of such credible sources is available and their critiques deserve careful attention. One was a respected twentieth-century historian, the other a singular theologian from earlier in the same century.

The early- and mid-twentieth-century enthusiasm for Luther studies, now dubbed the Luther Renaissance, produced a prodigious amount of literature on the reformer—some noteworthy and with enduring relevance, as evident from the previous chapter, some less helpful and with progressively diminishing value. Among the former, valuable, group of literature is a significant monograph from 1959 by F. Edward Cranz, complete with a reformation-esque title: *An Essay on the Development of Luther's Thought on Justice, Law, and Society.*[1] The bulk of the essay focuses on the centrality and consistency of Luther's twofold understanding of righteousness, or, as Cranz prefers to translate,

---

1. F. Edward Cranz, *An Essay on the Development of Luther's Thought on Justice, Law, and Society* (Mifflinton, PA: Sigler Press, 1998).

justice, for all of Luther's theology. The essay is a significant and important contribution to the ongoing discussion about the two kinds of righteousness, but also relevant, albeit tangentially, to the present question. As Cranz fulfills the objective prescribed in the latter part of his title, he corroborates my previous chapter's argument for a full and faithful reading of Luther that is manifest in a more aggressive and lively interaction between the two realms—which, though related, should not be confused with twofold justice. Cranz describes the relationship between the two different paradigms this way: "In broad outline God's spiritual government is comparable to passive justice in the heavenly realm while His world-government is comparable to civil justice and the civil use of the law in the world."[2] Of course, the critical point for Luther, as Cranz recognizes, is that "all Christians must exist in two realms and are thus subject both to God's spiritual government and also to His world-government."[3] When it comes to the two realms, then, both are from God, and both are good—even for the Christian.

Overall, the work of Cranz is significant and quite valuable, but while the bulk of his essay serves nicely as corroboration and contribution to my present thesis, it also succeeds in posing a sharp challenge to the same—the challenge commonly raised that calls into question the continuing relevance of Luther's thought for the contemporary world. In the last three paragraphs of his substantive (and lengthy) essay, Cranz raises the question of the applicability of Luther's thinking and teaching on the two realms in cultures that are not operating under the direct influence of Christian teaching and leadership. Highlighting the reformer's doctrine of the three estates or hierarchies and their impact on Luther's world, Cranz moves from the limits of historical evaluation and observes, "One cannot, to my knowledge, find in Luther the extension of the three hierarchies to a non-Christian society, and we must therefore be cautious in relating the hierarchies to the non-Christian categories of reason and polity."[4] A paragraph later, Cranz writes, "Luther develops a theology of the world only for Christians

---

2. Ibid., 168.
3. Ibid., 172.
4. Ibid., 176. The three estates referenced by Cranz are home, state, and church.

in a Christian society; he affirms a Christian secularization and not a secularization without qualification."[5] One could be forgiven for concluding that Cranz most certainly limits the applicability of Luther's two realms schema to cultures that are wholly or at least recognizably Christian. It seems that Cranz says nothing less. And, if this reading of Cranz is accurate and the challenge prevails, then in quick succession, many dominoes begin to fall.

First, if it is true that Luther's teaching on the two realms is only fit and meaningful for a Christian society, then it is evident that in great swaths of the world, those areas relatively untouched by Christian influence, Luther's two realms must be ruled out of bounds, and so, considered irrelevant and pointless—the reformer has nothing to contribute. Further, if the challenge raised by Cranz is right, what then of a nation founded on the virtue of the nonestablishment of any religion, including Christianity? In a setting like this, with its practiced neutrality toward Christian confession, it would seem clear that Luther's ideas would be far from compelling and without merit. Still more concerning for my thesis is the situation, now in full bloom in North America, when ties between the culture and Christianity that were once natural, robust, and happily cultivated—even if not officially sanctioned—are resolutely dissolved and deliberately severed at an accelerating pace. The American culture has undergone some significant changes in the last decades. If Luther's teaching depends on a Christian society, then the contemporary relevance and importance of that teaching in the United States clearly seems dubious at best. Of course, this truth applies also to those Western nations that maintain an official Christian church, yet present a culture that could be dubbed Christian only in a decidedly vague or exceedingly generous sense of the word. Indeed, if the claim voiced by Cranz is right and Luther's teaching only holds in a society akin to Luther's, it would seem that in the twenty-first-century world, there is essentially no country on earth that qualifies as a fit locale for the practice of the Wittenberger's social teaching. Which is precisely how some, even those otherwise

5. Ibid., 177.

supportive of Luther's teaching, are inclined to assess the contemporary suitability and significance of the reformer's "political" teaching. Apparently, in view of the dramatic disjunction between Luther's world and our own, it seems self-evident that the teaching of the two realms requires either significant revision or rejection altogether, and Cranz gives voice to this point of view.

The Applicability of Luther

It might be wise to return here to the beginning of our hypothetical column of pip-marked tiles. While extending his discussion about the necessary presence of a Christian society as the context for Luther's social teaching, Cranz actually advances in a different direction than the hypothetical critics of Luther's political thinking represented by the previous paragraph's queue of toppling dominoes:

> Indeed, from Luther's standpoint, we never find any true secularization apart from Christianity, for only Christianity teaches us not to "mix" the two realms, which the natural man cannot even distinguish. Apart from Christianity, what ought to be the world or reason or polity will always falsely claim to be more than the world, to be in some way a means of salvation, or a stage on the way to heaven, or a "church."[6]

This reveals the critical point, and keeps the first domino upright. It is not that Cranz is suggesting severe limits on the validity, veracity, or even applicability of Luther's teaching. He is certainly not saying that Luther's teaching is true or useful only in a medieval Constantinian context. He is not suggesting that a non-Christian society demands a different paradigm or approach. Cranz does not make such a claim. His point, rather, is that Christians alone are capable of grasping the full depth and breadth of the wonder and the beauty implicit in Luther's doctrine of the two realms. Without Christian faith, fallen human beings always create their own heavens, paths of salvation, and institutions of spirituality, in the only way available: by wrongly elevating the status and value of the temporal into the eternal. The

6. Ibid.

point Cranz makes is actually rather self-evident: outside of Christian faith, it is quite impossible to apprehend the truth about the world, hence only Christians are able rightly to appropriate their place in the world. It is not that Luther's ideas are no longer true or effective in a non-Christian society, it is simply that there is no way that they can be broadly heard much less usefully implemented in a non-Christian society. In such settings, they can only appear as sectarian nonsense.

This is a vital clarification and subsequent distinction. If Luther's "doctrine of the two kingdoms" is simply the attempt of one late medieval dropout from monasticism to analyze and systematize his own immediate world situation, then it has little more than historical value and should occupy the attention of only the smallest handful of one of the most obscure and arcane corners of the academy. However, if Luther's teaching about God's twofold rule in the world is a correct presentation of God's eternal truth—which is, of course, the very definition of true systematic theology—then it is valid and applicable in all places at all times and for all people. The difference cannot be more profound. Cranz may not explicitly endorse the second position, but neither does he support or even suggest the first. It is not his purpose to address the question of whether Luther's teaching is true; rather, he is content to explore the content and potential meaning of that teaching. So, while there may be those who claim that Luther's social teaching has nothing to offer a contemporary world that bears so little resemblance to the reformer's long lost Christian society, Cranz, it turns out, cannot be claimed as their champion.

Distinguishing Luther from Lutheran Heresy

The Luther historian has been heard and examined, now attention turns to the other half of my representative pair of critics: the theologian who is knowledgeable, yet appears to disapprove of Luther's political thought. One of the reformer's heirs who is routinely counted in the category of "Lutheran, yet nevertheless critical of Luther's twofold distinction" is Dietrich Bonhoeffer. Franklin Sherman can expect little argument when he asserts about the "two kingdoms doctrine": "theologians such as Barth and Bonhoeffer have condemned the doctrine as the source of a hopeless dualism and defeatism."[7] Barth's contempt for Luther's distinction between the realms is no secret, but Bonhoeffer's own critical assessment may be less widely known. The assertion that Bonhoeffer spurned the doctrine of the two kingdoms is not without supporting evidence; nevertheless, a bit more nuance may be in order than that suggested by Sherman's confident claim. Of course, there is no doubt that Bonhoeffer made some sharp comments highly critical of any attempt at establishing two spheres or realms, "one divine, holy, supernatural, and Christian; the other worldly, profane, natural, and unchristian."[8] This distinction, Bonhoeffer contends, became dominant in the Middle Ages, and then, again after the Reformation. For Bonhoeffer, the essential problem with this division is its failure to see all of reality subsumed within and under Jesus Christ. With the comprehensive understanding of Jesus over all that is endorsed by Bonhoeffer, one can "never experience the reality of God without the reality of the world nor the reality of the world without the reality of God."[9] This beautiful and powerful truth, Bonhoeffer believes, is abandoned when the duality is established:

> This division of the whole of reality into sacred and profane, or Christian and worldly, sectors creates the possibility of existence in only one of the sectors: for instance, a spiritual existence that takes no part in worldly existence, and a worldly existence that can make good its claim to autonomy over against the sacred sector.[10]

At this juncture, Bonhoeffer seems indeed to be solidly on the side of those condemning Luther's doctrine. But, there is more to the argument.

It is quite true that Bonhoeffer is greatly alarmed at the dangers of the bifurcation, and so, asserts the contrary truth with zeal: "There

7. Franklin Sherman, "Introduction," in Heinrich Bornkamm, *Luther's Doctrine of the Two Kingdoms in the Context of His Theology* (Philadelphia, PA: Fortress Press, 1966), iii.
8. Dietrich Bonhoeffer, *Ethics*, vol. 6 in *Dietrich Bonhoeffer Works*, ed. Clifford J. Green, trans. Reinhard Krauss, Charles C. West, and Douglas W. Stott (Minneapolis, MN: Fortress Press, 2009), 56.
9. Ibid., 55.
10. Ibid., 57.

are not two realities, but only one reality, and that is the reality of God, which has become manifest in Christ in the reality of the world. Sharing in Christ we stand at once in both the reality of God and the reality of the world."[11] Bonhoeffer will go even further and explicitly deny the possibility of two spheres. He writes, "Hence there are not two realms, but only *the one realm of the Christ-reality [Christuswirklichkeit]*, in which the reality of God and the reality of the world are united."[12] Conclusive as this seems, it is important to hear Bonhoeffer's introductory thought to these strong statements. "As hard as it may now seem to break the spell of this conceptual framework of realms," he notes, "it is just as certain that this perspective deeply contradicts both biblical and Reformation thought, therefore bypassing reality."[13] It is the word *Reformation*, of course, which is perhaps unexpected and so vitally significant. Bonhoeffer does not fault the Reformation, or at least, the vital force of the Reformation, with the dualistic error. Indeed, Bonhoeffer, it is clear, actually endorses Luther's thinking, with the stipulation that Luther be rightly understood and used. Recognizing the importance of this point, it is worth hearing Bonhoeffer at some length:

> As Luther polemically led the worldly battle against the sacralizing trend of the Roman church, so this worldliness must be polemically contradicted by the Christian, by the "sacred," in the very moment when it is in danger of making itself independent, as happened soon after the Reformation, reaching its high point in cultural Protestantism. The issue in both cases is precisely the same, namely referring to the reality of God and the reality of the world in Jesus Christ. In the name of a better Christianity Luther used the worldly to protest against a type of Christianity that was making itself independent by separating itself from the reality in Christ. Similarly, Christianity must be used polemically today against the worldly in the name of a better worldliness; this polemical use of Christianity must not end up again in a static and self-serving sacred realm. Only in this sense of a polemical unity may Luther's doctrine of the two kingdoms [Zwei Reiche] be used. That was probably its original meaning.[14]

11. Ibid., 58 (italics in original).
12. Ibid. (italics in original).
13. Ibid.
14. Ibid., 59–60.

Bonhoeffer rightly understood that the problem is not Luther or Luther's teaching or even Luther's "doctrine of two kingdoms." The problem is the perversion and misuse of his teaching.

This contrast between Luther's teaching and the misappropriation of that teaching masquerading as a faithful presentation of Luther's thought has been recognized by a number of Lutheran theologians. Aware of Karl Barth's vigorous condemnation of the doctrine—the great Swiss theologian is given credit for coining the moniker "two-kingdoms doctrine" as a slight against the teaching—Robert Benne, nevertheless, argues that even this critique is directed not at Luther, but at the misuse of Luther.[15] Benne describes this wrong teaching, the object of Barth's scorn, as a dualistic approach: "According to this dualistic model, which is a Lutheran heresy, there are two completely separate spheres, one having to do with earthly society and the other having to do with the salvation of our souls."[16] The point not to be overlooked is Benne's forthright and accurate declaration that the errant teaching is heresy—a heresy to which Lutherans seem to have a peculiar vulnerability. Ulrich Duchrow also derides the misappropriation of Luther's teaching. He blames "liberal-bourgeois Lutheranism" for establishing "the theoretical justification of the notorious concept that the spheres of life are autonomous."[17] He precedes Benne in labeling this falsification of Luther's teaching "an anti-Christian heresy."[18] There is a marked difference, then, between the teaching of Luther, and the teaching that would neatly bifurcate the spiritual and the temporal spheres. The former conforms to orthodox truth; the latter is simply heresy.

Much more is at stake here, however, than a scholarly exercise more accurately to assign blame for false teaching, or the even more trivial (and as usual, unnecessary) desire to provide a spirited defense of the great reformer. Far more important is the need for the church rightly

---

15. Robert Benne, *The Paradoxical Vision: A Public Theology for the Twenty-First Century* (Minneapolis, MN: Fortress Press, 1995), 79.
16. Ibid.
17. Duchrow, *Lutheran Churches*, 13.
18. Ibid., 292.

to hear, appreciate, and practice the actual teaching of scripture and its student, Luther, on the place of the world in Christian thinking. Toward this end, Bonhoeffer proves to be of inestimable value. Penetrating and complex as Bonhoeffer can be in his analysis of doctrinal truths, the premise guiding his thinking on the Christian's relation to the world is quite simple. Christ is all in all and over all, thus the Christian must indulge in a robust engagement with the world since it is thoroughly Christ's world. To confess faith in Christ is to endorse the world as good, and so, worthy of the investment of diligent work. There is no possibility that a faithful Christian can forsake her involvement in the world. Bonhoeffer deftly outlines the progression from faith in Christ to commitment to the world:

> Since ethical thinking in terms of realms is overcome by faith in the revelation of ultimate reality in Jesus Christ, it follows that there is no real Christian existence outside the reality of the world and no real worldliness outside the reality of Jesus Christ. For the Christian there is nowhere to retreat from the world, neither externally nor into the inner life. Every attempt to evade the world will have to be paid for sooner or later with a sinful surrender to the world.[19]

The Christian's investment in the world is not an endorsement or uncritical acceptance and approval of the world—far from it. Rather, the Christian is fully invested in the world and the world's affairs, structures, and institutions in order to accomplish God's purposes for the world and to bring every part of the world more fully in harmony with the Creator's will and design.

Bonhoeffer is opposed, then, not to Luther's teaching on the distinction of the two realms or spheres. He is opposed to the thinking that would set these spheres against each other or partition them into separate and isolated realms. They must be held together because in Christ, they simply are together. Following Luther, Bonhoeffer is at liberty to draw a sharp contrast between God and the world, or using Luther's terminology, between things spiritual and things temporal. Yet, also in line with Luther, Bonhoeffer stresses that these two distinct

19. Bonhoeffer, *Ethics*, 61.

areas of God's action are tightly bound—bound beneath the lordship and the salvation of Christ. This truth drives the believer in Christ never into solitude or retreat from the world, but always into the community of life together for the sake of the world. Further, the inextricable union of the two realities in and under the one great reality of Jesus brings concord and coherence to the life of the Christian. Bonhoeffer completely stifles the reproach of those who would accuse Luther's teaching of creating schizophrenic or at least maladjusted Christian people torn by dueling allegiances:

> Whoever confesses the reality of Jesus Christ as the revelation of God confesses in the same breath the reality of God and the reality of the world, for they find God and the world reconciled in Christ. Just for this reason the Christian is no longer the person of eternal conflict. As reality is *one* in Christ, so the person who belongs to this Christ-reality is also a whole. Worldliness does not separate one from Christ, and being Christian does not separate one from the world. Belonging completely to Christ, one stands at the same time completely in the world.[20]

A Christian, then, is to be altogether worldly—committed to and enmeshed in the affairs of the world all around her, and simultaneously, and indeed consequently, centered squarely in the will of God. She lives continually in two quite distinct spheres, yet never as a divided or conflicted person, but as a unified and complete individual well aware of the twofold reality in which she lives. Bonhoeffer's teaching, here, is in full accord with that of the great reformer.

Cranz and Bonhoeffer, then, are not at odds with those who believe that Luther's teaching on the two realms continues to apply to the world of the twenty-first century. My own position on the continued relevance should be quite apparent, but in the ongoing interest of transparency, I will be explicit: I contend that Luther's teaching is an entirely accurate articulation of God's limitless and timeless truth. That puts it in a very different category than other social or political thinking. Luther's social teaching is not just one more artifact in the ponderously long succession of history's political theorists that can be

20. Ibid., 62.

studied, adopted, adapted, dismissed, or disparaged according to the inclinations of the individual. Rather, the core of Luther's social and political teaching is an integral part of his overall theological teaching. And since it is a matter of theological confession, I contend that such teaching is thus never an issue subject to personal preference or academic debate. It is, at its heart, God's reality at work in the world, and so, universally binding, relevant, and appropriate. Naturally, such teaching commands the careful attention of all who seek faithfully to follow a Christian confession; at the very least, it should enjoy the favor of those who are the immediate heirs of Luther's determined effort faithfully to express that confession.

The fundamental challenge, calling into question the continuing suitability and relevance of Luther's teaching for the contemporary situation, has been met and dispatched. And in the process of sorting out Bonhoeffer's thinking on the question, the course of this book's unfolding argument has been fortified with an additional, unsought gift. Bonhoeffer's trenchant and bracing interpretation of Luther brilliantly articulates and advances my own thesis of the enduring importance of Luther's actual teaching for the church today. His interpretation and application of two realms thinking enhances the overall appreciation of Luther's teaching, and so, deserves careful attention. The remainder of this chapter, then, will endeavor to listen to Bonhoeffer and further enrich both the understanding and practice of the teaching of the two realms in the church today.

Bonhoeffer Addresses the Church

Bonhoeffer's thinking has much to say to individual Christian believers as well as to the church as a whole about what it means to live faithfully in and toward the world. To appreciate Bonhoeffer's argument, it must be remembered that in the whole of creation, Christ incarnate is the one great truth and foundation of all things. "When God in Jesus Christ claims space in the world—even space in a stable because 'there was no other place in the inn'—God embraces the whole reality of the world in this narrow space and reveals its ultimate foundation."[21] Thus,

Christians who live in Christ live simultaneously in both realities, or as Bonhoeffer puts it, "Partaking in Christ, we stand at the same time in the reality of God and in the reality of the world in itself."[22] The church, then, is concerned not only with the reality of God's things—things commonly considered "spiritual," but also with the reality that is the world. And in its relationship to the world, the church has a specific task to fulfill. It becomes the locus of God's witness in and to the world, "that is, the space [Raum]—in the world," writes Bonhoeffer, "where the reign of Jesus Christ over the whole world is to be demonstrated and proclaimed."[23] The church is not in competition with the world, not a mirror reflection of the world, and not the fawning and aping little brother of the world. Rather, it exists distinct from the world for the good of the world, to serve the world by declaring to the world the reality and the reign of Christ.

While there is potentially a hazard of this discussion becoming drastically sidetracked at this point with a discussion of ecclesiology and the identity and purpose of the church, it is a risk that needs to be accepted. To understand Bonhoeffer's insights into the interface of church and world, one must first appreciate his concept of the church. Bonhoeffer's approach to ecclesiology sets the stage for the position he develops regarding the church's relation to the world, including the state; further, it deserves careful consideration for the simple fact that Bonhoeffer's conception of the church is not one that most Christians today would readily recognize.

Whatever the reasons, noble or corrupt, legitimate or misguided, there is a notion among many believers in twenty-first-century America that the church exists as the antithesis to the world. Without using the terminology, this thinking amounts to a sort of gnostic approach to reality: the world is dark, material, futile, godless, and ultimately, a place of death; in stark contrast, the church is light, spiritual, meaningful, god-filled, and ultimately, a place of life. This thinking undergirds and explains much Christian thinking and

21. Ibid., 63.
22. Ibid., 58.
23. Ibid., 63.

behavior—from the desirability of establishing "Christian" versions of worldly activities, institutions, and practices (from plumbers to music to diet aids and movies) to dismissive and even fearful attitudes toward the world's science and scholarship. This way of conceiving the church is pervasive among Christians who would label themselves conservative. Another segment of Christians avoids such a gnostic view and considerably softens the antithesis in its understanding of the church as the one great reality that triumphs over all and rules over all, despite the world's failure to appreciate or even to recognize this. Still other believers, and there are far more of these than the previous sort, invert the order and subordinate the church to the great and grand things of the world—forsaking the antithesis altogether, the church becomes simply another unique and useful instrument at work in the world alongside a host of other such instruments, like the Red Cross, the United Way, the Sierra Club, and of course, any religion that proves meaningful to anyone for any reason.[24] Bonhoeffer's understanding of the church rejects all of these ways.

For Bonhoeffer, the church is not the polar antithesis to the world; it is not the equal and opposite counterbalancing force. Nor is the church the only reality that counts and the only divinely blessed and honored institution created by God to serve his purpose. But neither is the church one among many forces and institutions at work in the world for good or ill, vying for significance and influence in the public forum and in popular thought. No, in its fullest and truest identity, the

---

24. The perceptive reader may well detect the typology of H. Richard Niebuhr's classic, *Christ and Culture* at work in my three cursory characterizations. The correspondence to Niebuhr present in the previous paragraph could be evidence of that text on my thinking—or it may, more accurately I think, be a testimony to the insight and usefulness of Niebuhr's work, as his categories do seem to cohere with the reality I have briefly described, a reality that I believe is readily discerned by any alert observer of American Christians. I have no interest in entering an old debate either as a defender or a detractor of Niebuhr. My goal here is nothing more than to provide a representative sketch of some contemporary assumptions about the church that should be familiar and beyond dispute. By intention, my effort is far from exhaustive and is not meant to suggest a new typology to replace Niebuhr—in my opinion, this feat was already masterfully and convincingly accomplished by James D. Hunter (James Davison Hunter, *To Change the World: The Irony, Tragedy, and Possibility of Christianity in the Late Modern World* [Oxford: Oxford University Press, 2010]). Hunter's threefold division is well supported with extensive documentation, and every bit as useful and potentially fruitful as Niebuhr's older typology, and also maps, though rather loosely, to the three quick categories I have suggested.

church is not a human contrivance or a cultural artifact. It is God's creation, one of the two great realities that shape and define all that is. The church stands alongside the world not as its antithesis, but as its complement and servant—even as the world stands alongside the church as its complement and servant. The church does not eclipse the world, but illumines it. The church does not fight for its relevance or even its existence in the world. It exists by the will of God and is continually, inherently, and supremely relevant because it speaks to and from and for God. The church does not function in isolation for its own purpose; rather, all that it does, even its most peculiar, most other-worldly, and most spiritual acts and words are all for the sake of the world. Indeed, it is precisely the church's practices that are most disconnected from the routine and priorities of the world that the world most needs. The divine service with preaching, absolution, and the celebration of the Lord's Supper is the essential and most significant instance of the church's service to and for the world. All of this is at work in Bonhoeffer's conception of the church in the world.

The Church's Duality

Of course, Bonhoeffer would have been well aware of the critical and normative definitions of the church as expressed in the Book of Concord. "The church is the assembly of all believers among whom the Gospel is purely preached and the holy sacraments are administered according to the gospel."[25] God makes and maintains his church, his people, with the delivery of his gospel gifts. The idea that the church is, above all else, the *people* has become a commonplace in the thinking of most believers, one affirmed to some extent by Luther, "God be praised, a seven-year-old child knows what the church is: holy believers and 'the little sheep who hear the voice of their shepherd.'"[26] Yes, the church is sheep, that is, people, but not just any people, these are people who are hearing and heeding their shepherd. It is

---

25. Robert Kolb and Timothy Wengert, eds., *The Book of Concord: The Confessions of the Evangelical Lutheran Church* (Minneapolis, MN: Fortress Press, 2000), 42, AC VII, 1.
26. Ibid., 324–25, SA 3, 12, 2.

Melanchthon, in the Apology of the Augsburg Confession, who adds another—worldly—dimension to what the voice of the shepherd is telling these sheep about themselves: "However, the church is not only an association of external ties and rites like other civic organizations, but it is principally an association of faith and the Holy Spirit in the hearts of persons. It nevertheless has its external marks so that it can be recognized, namely, the pure teaching of the gospel and the administration of the sacraments in harmony with the gospel of Christ."[27] Granted, Melanchthon actually is stressing the opposite point, weighting the spirit and faith component; still, he takes for granted that the church is something more as well. It has a material side to it, complete with "external ties and rites," and in these external things, its identifying marks are to be found. The church, then, like her Lord, has a twofold identity.

The duality of the church's being is often expressed in terms of its visible and invisible aspects. An even more distracting digression into that conversation can be checked by turning to the good ecclesiastical work of Kurt Marquart, who recognized and resolved the danger of a twofold church degenerating into the errant thinking that would hold the existence of two churches. "To avoid suggesting this Calvinist dilemma of two churches," Marquart suggested, "it may be best when using the adjectives 'visible' and 'invisible,' to place them after the noun, i.e. 'church visible' and 'church invisible.' This linguistic device more readily conveys the idea that what is being described is not two churches but one and the same church in different respects."[28] This is sage counsel reflecting a much more profound and significant truth. Marquart captures the import of the deeper truth and tension quite well:

> To do justice to the bi-polarity or "complementarity" involved, we speak, with our Confessions, of the church in the proper sense (the believers as such) and of the same church in the wide sense (the believers gathered

27. Ibid., 174, Ap, VII/VIII, 5.
28. Kurt Marquart, *The Church and Her Fellowship, Ministry, and Governance*, vol. 9 of *Confessional Lutheran Dogmatics*, Robert D. Preus, ed. (Ft. Wayne, IN: The International Foundation for Lutheran Confessional Research, 1990), 24.

round the means of grace, plus the unbelieving hangers-on). In this way the doctrine of the church in its own way reflects the great incarnational and sacramental dimensions which shape the whole biblical evangel.[29]

All this is to say that a right and rich understanding of the church is always incarnational, sacramental, and ultimately, christological. The church is Christ's body, and like her Lord, has a spiritual, personal, invisible component and also a material, institutional, visible component. The two natures are not at odds. Neither are they loosely or nominally joined or ranked in some Nestorian way. There is one church: it is spiritual and certainly not part of this world, and it is material and certainly part of this world. This understanding of the church yields an abundant and wonderful harvest.

It is altogether impossible to disentangle, disconnect, or dissect the church's two aspects. By definition, they are joined in a union that is complete and complex. The church is an element in the world, one of the world's "parts," an institution with charters and constitutions and sociologically observable phenomena. But the church is also simultaneously the body of Christ, spiritual and quite apart from all that is in the world. Much as it is with good christological doctrine, one cannot push too hard here or demand precise and surpassing definitions that highlight one aspect, but inevitably diminish or delete some other essential aspect of the church's identity. By God's design, the church is in and *part of* the world, so it is always, according to its essence, temporal and earthly and messy. Yet, the church is also always purely and simply Christ's gospel being delivered and enacted by and for God's "heavenly citizens." This twofold nature of the church suffuses all that Bonhoeffer teaches about the church. Naturally, failing to recognize the truth of the two natures of the church, one may errantly assume that Bonhoeffer swings wildly between contradictory definitions. Bonhoeffer, though, is not guilty of doublespeak; he is merely faithful to the double nature of the church. Those who crave neat and comprehensive definitions, and who consistently betray their proclivities with questions such as, "Now, which church are we talking

29. Ibid.

about, the visible local church or the invisible universal church?" have thoroughly failed to grasp the right understanding of the church. The church's two natures cannot be atomized or parsed in this way without getting the church wrong. The church is its visible component—it is rituals and preaching and potlucks and politics. The church is its invisible component—it is union with Christ, forgiveness before God, perfect peace, and eternal life. The church transcends any one gathering or place, yet each single gathering or place is fully the church. All this is profoundly and riotously true of the church.[30]

The Church Engages the World

In the context of this rich and multifaceted conception of the church, one can more readily understand and appreciate Bonhoeffer's direction for the interrelation between the church and the world. Bonhoeffer makes two significant points prescribing the church's task toward the world, neither of which make a great deal of sense, apart from the previous description of the church. In a section worth quoting at length, Bonhoeffer specifies the church's responsibility in the world:

> The Church is the place where it is proclaimed and taken seriously that God has reconciled the world to himself in Christ, that God so loved the world that God gave his Son for it. The space of the church is not there in order to fight with the world for a piece of its territory, but precisely to testify to the world that it is still the world, namely, the world that is loved and reconciled by God. It is not true that the church intends to or must spread its space out over the space of the world. It desires no more space than it needs to serve the world with its witness to Jesus Christ and to the world's reconciliation to God through Jesus Christ. The church can only defend its own space by fighting, not for space, but for the salvation of the world. Otherwise the church becomes a "religious society" that fights in its own interest and thus has ceased to be the church of God in the world.[31]

---

30. The ontological and enduring unity of the church and its twofold nature should challenge, if not invalidate, all schemes to "clarify" one's referent for *church* by the use of upper and lower case letters or contrived use of definite articles. The distinction is arbitrary. "The Church" and "a church" are the same thing, ultimately; and whether an author or editor prefers the use of an upper or lower case *c* should be understood as theologically irrelevant and meaningless. Either way, there remains but one church.
31. Bonhoeffer, *Ethics*, 63–64.

The church is not trying to conquer or win the world. The church is not trying to suppress or stymie the world. The church seeks merely to witness to the world of the reconciliation of Christ, and thereby, to save the world. It hardly seems hyperbole to suggest that were the members of the church to arrive at this self-understanding, the result could only be revolutionary for both church and world. Indeed, the import of Bonhoeffer's clear expression of the church's purpose deserves greater consideration and will shape the work of the next chapter.

It would be a mistake, though, to conclude that a church that exists to witness to the reconciliation of Christ is timid, retiring, and deferential. The opposite is the case. As the place that practices and delivers the redemptive activity of God for the sake of the world, the church must act with a courage and assertiveness that almost certainly would alarm many both outside and inside the church. Neither does the church simply whisper love songs and sweet consolations to the world. As necessary, it confronts and rebukes the world. The world must know that Christ is Lord not only of the church, but also of the world. Bonhoeffer makes this clear:

> Christ as the salvation of the world means the dominion of Christ over persons and things. Here the dominion of Christ means something different for individual persons than it does, e.g., for the state, economics, etc. It is only through the dominion of Christ that all things—the human being, the state, the economy, etc.—first arrive at their true being. But all these things belong together and may not be arbitrarily torn apart.[32]

Within God's great design for his creation, every part, every person, every institution has its peculiar role, and can rightly fulfill that role only as it conforms to the intention of the Creator. The world must know this truth. As those particularly interested in God's truth, it falls to the church to shoulder the responsibility of making known the will of God for his creation. Bonhoeffer discusses this in the context of the first, or norming, use of the law, which he labels *primus usus*: "With the *primus usus* the Church testifies that it does not abandon the world to

---

32. Dietrich Bonhoeffer, *Conspiracy and Imprisonment: 1940-1945*, vol. 16 in *Dietrich Bonhoeffer Works*, ed. Mark S. Brocker, trans. Lisa E. Dahill (Minneapolis, MN: Fortress Press, 2006), 543.

itself but calls it to come under the dominion of Christ."[33] As part of the creation, the world must live in obedience to the will of God as revealed in the law or the commandments of God. The concern of the first use of the law is "with the worldly orders themselves according to God's will—not with Christianizing [Verchristlichung] or making them more like the Church [Verkirchlichung], i.e., the abrogation of the 'relative' autonomy of worldly orders, but with their genuine worldliness, 'naturalness' in obedience to God's Word."[34] The world is the world, and is not the church; yet, it is God's world. And that world must live in accord with God's Word, and the church must be committed to helping the world be the world rightly related to its Creator, no matter how difficult or unpleasant that task may be for the church to undertake.

The coherence between Luther's teaching on God's two realms of operation, the temporal and the spiritual, and Bonhoeffer's emphasis on God's twofold rule over both church and world should be convincingly apparent. Any suggestion that Bonhoeffer rejected or substantially modified Luther's teaching simply does not square with the facts. Even in the arena of church and state and their interrelationship, Bonhoeffer taught not only in the spirit of the reformer but the content of the reformer. Bonhoeffer's consistency in teaching in agreement with Luther can be seen also in his careful instruction about the Christian in relationship to the divisions of life: home, state, and church. Of course, it is widely recognized that Luther made frequent use of these medieval categories of the three hierarchies or estates. Cranz cites a bundle of disputations, commentaries, and essays from late in Luther's career in which the reformer affirms that "God ordained three hierarchies against the devil, that is the household, the polity, and the church."[35] Through the activities and accomplishments of the home, including one's work in support of that home, the state or government, and finally, the church, each person finds her appropriate and particular avenue of work and service for the good of the surrounding creation, and thus,

---

33. Ibid., 546.
34. Ibid.
35. Cranz, *An Essay*, 175.

to the detriment of Satan's kingdom. As Cranz rightly summarizes, Luther's peculiar use of the hierarchies emphasized that "none of the three hierarchies is a 'spiritual rule' in the old [i.e., medieval Roman Catholicism] sense but that all of them, even 'secular rule,' are holy."[36] Further, Cranz notes that as Luther used the terms, not only are all three holy, but at the same time, all three are also completely worldly in that they are arenas of activity for the good of the world. Bonhoeffer certainly would have been aware of this familiar threefold approach toward understanding life in terms of distinct arenas of responsibility. In fact, he takes them and uses them to form the framework for his own practical teaching on the subject.

The Four Mandates

Bonhoeffer's expansion of the three estates comes in his development of what he names the four mandates, discussed at the end of his essay "Christ, Reality, and Good," a pivotal chapter in his *Ethics* and already sourced above for much of his thinking on the interrelationship of church and state. The German theologian introduces his subject this way:

> Like all of creation, the world has been created through Christ and toward Christ and has its existence only in Christ (John 1:10; Col 1:16). To speak of the world without speaking of Christ is pure abstraction. The world stands in relationship to Christ whether the world knows it or not. This relation of the world to Christ becomes concrete in certain *mandates of God* in the world. The scripture names four such mandates: *work, marriage, government, and church.*[37]

Bonhoeffer's subsequent presentation of the import and extent of the idea of the four mandates is worthy of careful consideration here for at least two reasons. First, while, Bonhoeffer is rightly troubled by those who would use the three estates neatly to split the world into discrete and unrelated spheres or, even worse, to split a person into three disconnected roles, it is instructive to note how there is a strong

36. Ibid., 176.
37. Bonhoeffer, *Ethics*, 68 (italics original).

correlation between Luther's understanding and practice of the estates and his twentieth-century heir's treatment of the mandates. What Bonhoeffer presents is not at variance but altogether compatible with what Luther actually taught and did. Second, Bonhoeffer's brief teaching on this subject is invaluable for a right grasp of the relation between the temporal and spiritual realms and will prove exceedingly useful when the practical significance and implications of Luther's teaching are considered in the chapters to follow. Since the present chapter has already explored Bonhoeffer's contribution to a right understanding of the legitimacy and relevance of the distinctive Lutheran teaching on the two realms, to hear him now on the topic of the mandates is altogether appropriate.

In typical fashion, Bonhoeffer expresses the substance of his thesis immediately and simply. Christ is all in all and all four mandates are caught up in this singular reality. "In the world," continues Bonhoeffer, "God wills work, marriage, government, and church, and God wills all these, each in its own way, through Christ, toward Christ, and in Christ."[38] The mandates are God's provision for the accomplishment of his purposes in the world. Through them, his plan—which is manifest in Christ and consummated in the work of Christ—is brought forward to the day of fulfillment. All four mandates apply to all persons. There is no division into three or four parts; there is no conflict within the world or the person. "God has placed human beings under all these mandates," Bonhoeffer teaches, "not only each individual under one or the other, but all people under all four."[39] To varying extents, then, and with different emphases in relation to their particular responsibilities, all persons are engaged in all of the mandates. Bonhoeffer rightly understands that the mandates are never mutually exclusive or practiced in isolation. Every person, regardless of her role or status in work, home, state, and church, should be interested in each of the four mandates, and in fact, has peculiar responsibilities in each of the four mandates. In her exercise of the mandates, a person does

38. Ibid., 69.
39. Ibid.

not experience disjunction or struggle between them. As Bonhoeffer insists, the first three mandates "are not there to divide people and tear them apart but to deal with them as whole people before God, the Creator, Reconciler, and Redeemer."[40] It is when the person lives rightly before God that each distinct mandate is correctly juxtaposed with the others. "The divine mandates in the world are not there to wear people down through endless conflicts. Rather, they aim," Bonhoeffer explains, "at the whole human being who stands in reality before God."[41] This understanding of the continuity and complementarity of the mandates stands in line with Luther's own teaching on the subject.

The specific teaching on each of the first three mandates is presented without great surprise or remarkable departure from expected explanations. Labor is grounded in the creation account, and so, begins with the work assigned to the first person. Not to be missed, is the obvious fact that such a grounding eliminates any erroneous idea of work as inherently inhumane or an aspect of a cursed existence. Work is integral to human being and flourishing: "The work founded in paradise calls for cocreative human deeds. Through them a world of things and values is created that is destined for the glory and service of Jesus Christ."[42] From the tasks of tending the garden and tilling the fields, this work expands out and up to include "the invention of violins and flutes, which give us on earth a foretaste of heavenly music."[43] Man's labor also finds appropriate expression in other artistic and skilled endeavors:

> Then comes the extraction and processing of metallic treasures dug out of the earth, partly to decorate the earthly house like the heavenly city that shines with gold and precious stones, and partly to make swords of avenging justice. Through the divine mandate of work, a world should emerge that—knowingly or unknowingly—expects Christ, is directed toward Christ, is open for Christ, and serves and glorifies Christ.[44]

40. Ibid., 73.
41. Ibid.
42. Ibid., 70.
43. Ibid., 71.
44. Ibid.

This passage contains several noteworthy moves. It accentuates the tight connection Bonhoeffer consistently makes between the world as we know it and the eschatological fulfillment that waits ahead as the telos of this world. For Bonhoeffer, the material world with its flutes and gilding is not a temporary home or prison for spiritual beings. The world is the place of God's activity and the great work of his creative hand. It is a world to be cultivated and celebrated. Of course, such a view is readily found also in the work of Bonhoeffer's foremost teacher, Luther.

Two further points should be gleaned from Bonhoeffer's summary thoughts about the mandate quoted in the previous paragraph. Within the present economy of God's purpose for this world, Bonhoeffer rightly recognizes a place for the sword. Justice is a godly virtue and a pursuit pleasing to the Creator. Of course, the sword was unnecessary in the pristine world of Eden. But, with man's rebellion and the entry of evil into God's good creation, the enforcement of justice was required. Justice and the state that will administer this justice are not anomalous to the purposes of God. They are, in fact, required for the accomplishment of God's sweeping purpose for his creation. With the sword, the creation is preserved for a time, awaiting the day of fulfillment when perfect justice will be realized and the need for swords finally eliminated. But, this point can be given further attention when it reappears under the mandate of the government. The other point not to be missed is Bonhoeffer's confident assertion of the intrinsic value of all labor done for the sake of the world, regardless of the motives or intentions of the worker. Whatever is done in the world to advance beauty, wisdom, health, fellowship, and human flourishing is done within the scope of God's messianic plan put into action and brought at last to consummation by his Christ. The worker works for God even in spite of himself. Through human labor God's plan is advanced and his purposes prevail.

The Shadow over the Mandates

Bonhoeffer does not conclude his consideration on such a high and optimistic note, however. Before starting fresh with the next mandate, Bonhoeffer's last word is a sad and sober observation: "That the descendants of Cain should fulfill this mandate casts a deep shadow over all human work."[45] The progeny of fallen Adam proves that not even fratricide lies beyond the reach of rebellious man, and so, Cain falls hopelessly short of the messianic expectations of his parents. It is the heirs of Cain, Bonhoeffer reminds us, who work in this world, and consequently, no work is free of the spreading stain of Cain. Such a disjunctive thought would seem to negate all the theologian's previous lofty conceptions and descriptions of human work in concert with the mission of Christ. But that is precisely the point, of course—and once again, wholly congruent with the thought and writing of Luther. There is nothing simple or transparent about human labor. Every bit of it is complicated by a bifurcated reality. God is the source and the norm of all labor—and the one who will collect and complete all that labor into an exultant festival of creation on the day of Christ's return. Yet, the same labor that propels, cultivates, and adorns the world is polluted always with egocentricity, avarice, apathy, hatred, and a steadily expanding catalog of human perversity. It is never simply one or the other. The human being works and does her work, whether consciously or not, for and in Christ always, yet even for that work, one must repent always.

Marriage or the home is the next mandate succinctly explained by Bonhoeffer. Like labor, marriage is grounded in the account of creation, and like labor, marriage is, since the fall, profoundly bifurcated. "By participating in creating [mitschaffend], human beings enter into the will of the Creator," writes Bonhoeffer.[46] And in this blessed estate, the children born are then to be raised "for the glory and service of Jesus Christ and the enlarging of Christ's kingdom."[47]

45. Ibid.
46. Ibid., 71.
47. Ibid.

So, marriage includes also the holy responsibility of parents to educate and form their children to be all that the Creator intends, "into obedience to Jesus Christ."[48] Still, this lofty and ennobling property of marriage is severely tempered. Like Adam's first son, Cain, all other sons and daughters of human parents are born "far from paradise," so "here, too, a dark shadow falls over marriage and family in this our world."[49] In this broken world, marriage is never quite what the Creator intended. Yet, neither is it beyond the reach of his grace and purposes.

Resting on the mandates of labor and marriage, the mandate of government is, in a sense, derivative, depending entirely on the creative aspects of home and work. The government is not a producer or creator of life or the goods in life. About government, Bonhoeffer bluntly asserts: "It is not creative." Rather, the work of government is preservation: "Government protects what is created by establishing justice in acknowledgement of the divine mandates and by enforcing this justice with the power of the sword."[50] For Bonhoeffer, then, the role of government is quite limited and circumscribed, and he takes a decidedly conservative approach to government and its purposes. Government does not create or advance marriage, but witnesses and guarantees it. Government does not administer "the great spheres of work" but inspects and supervises its conduct. All this is done within the grand plan of the Creator for his world: "By establishing justice, and by the power of the sword, government preserves the world for the reality of Jesus Christ."[51] And because the government, even unwittingly, is at work for the reality of Christ, even when using the sword, "Everyone owes obedience to this government—according to the will of Christ."[52] Living four hundred years after the reformer, Bonhoeffer may have become more wary of governments and their propensity for overreach and interference with the other mandates

48. Ibid.
49. Ibid.
50. Ibid., 72.
51. Ibid., 72–73.
52. Ibid., 73.

than was Luther; yet the agreement between the two on the place and role of government is certainly greater than the points of disparity.

The shift to the remaining mandate is marked by a singular change in tactic. Bonhoeffer departs from his established practice of highlighting the human being's specific responsibilities or tasks within the particular mandate, and then, accenting the brokenness and inadequacy which must always accompany any attempt to accomplish the work of that mandate. Instead, he begins his discussion of the mandate of the church by acknowledging that there is a marked difference, indeed a contrast, between the first three mandates and the final one. "In contrast to the three mandates named above, the divine mandate of the church is the commission of allowing the reality of Jesus Christ to become real in proclamation [Verkündigung], church order, and Christian life."[53] In Bonhoeffer's way of understanding God's mandates, the work of the church is "enabling the reality of Jesus Christ to become real in the preaching and organization of the Church and Christian life."[54] As always, Christ stands at the beginning, center, and end of Bonhoeffer's theology. To be faithful to the divine mandate, the church must make this Christ-reality apparent and tangible in the world where the other mandates are in action. How exactly this might happen, Bonhoeffer does not explore here—though in his other writings, it becomes clear enough what he has in mind for both the believer and the church.[55] It is possible, then, to detect a progression with the four mandates. Labor imposes itself on every person and cares directly for the creation. Marriage provides an arena, direction, and support for one's labor. Government, in turn, oversees and guarantees the space necessary for labor and marriage rightly to function. And finally, the church infiltrates and fills all the mandates with the reality of Christ present in every mandate. Thus, the scope of this fourth mandate is not limited only to the tasks it undertakes within its own

---

53. Ibid.
54. Ibid.
55. In *Life Together*, the picture of a community of faith holding one another responsible to the tasks of their individual and communal callings is presented in ways that are altogether concrete. And in *The Cost of Discipleship*, Bonhoeffer provides a fuller picture of the reality of Jesus as it impacts the person who would heed the call of Christ and follow the Lord faithfully.

immediate purview. It includes everything. "In short," Bonhoeffer continues, "its concern is the eternal salvation of the whole world."[56] Consequently, it is concerned with the right practice and concrete realization of each of the first three mandates. The church does not cloister itself in a religious corner, gaze heavenward, and contemplate only what is pure and spiritual. It is, on the contrary, altogether interested and invested in the function of the other mandates as they guide and serve the world.

Notwithstanding all that the final mandate has to say to the church, it applies in fact not only to the church but to every person. "The mandate of the church embraces all people, and it does so within all the other mandates."[57] Merely by virtue of his creation, every person is obligated to fulfill his tasks within all four mandates. Unless rightly oriented to his Creator through the Church—that is through Christ manifest in the fourth mandate—a person is not able rightly to realize any of the mandates. And so, the church occupies a place that is uniquely comprehensive in its scope and interest—an inclusive sweep not present in the other mandates. The unity of one's creaturely existence is bound together, then, with the work of the fourth mandate as that mandate is fulfilled both by the church and by the individual creature. Bonhoeffer puts it this way:

> Since a person is at the same time worker, spouse, and citizen, since one mandate overlaps with the others, and since all the mandates need to be fulfilled at the same time, so the church mandate reaches into all the other mandates. Similarly, the Christian is at the same time worker, spouse, and citizen. Every division into separate realms [Räume] is forbidden here. Human beings as whole persons stand before the whole earthly and eternal reality that God in Jesus Christ has prepared for them.[58]

When it is doing its God-ordained task, the church brings the reality of Christ into the reality of each person, and that human life is then transformed and shaped into the specificity and significance of God incarnate in Christ. This is eternal salvation: conformity to and

56. Bonhoeffer, *Ethics*, 73.
57. Ibid.
58. Ibid.

participation in God's plan of creation, restoration, and consummation. This is the reality of Christ. Bonhoeffer is ably describing the dynamic of the Christian walk lived out within two distinct spheres—the believer celebrates the tasks of work, family, and government as divine duties done for the good of the surrounding creation; and simultaneously, the believer does this labor in the certain knowledge of his right standing before his Creator through the faithful work of Christ who gives and sustains faith and provides grace and strength for the responsibilities of earthly existence articulated in the mandates. Not surprisingly, this entire presentation of Bonhoeffer, it should be readily apparent, is wholly compatible with the thought expressed by both St. Paul and Martin Luther.

When a Mandate Falters

One final point in Bonhoeffer's treatment of the mandates bears consideration before turning to the practical and potentially more interesting task of applying Luther's teaching to the world of Western civilization in the early twenty-first century. Bonhoeffer is not naïve, idealistic, or romantic about these worldly mandates and their fulfillment. Indeed, he lauds them as God's own mandates and celebrates the good that comes from and through them according to God's plan, but he also confronts the possibility that a specific instance of one of the mandates could fall short of the divine intention.

> Not because there *is* work, marriage, government, or church is it *commanded* by God, but because it is *commanded* by God, therefore it *is*. Only insofar as its being is subjected—consciously or unconsciously—to the divine task is it a divine mandate. In the concrete case, persistent, arbitrary violation of this task through concrete forms of work, marriage, government, and church extinguishes the divine mandate.[59]

It is not that the actual reality that purports to be the mandate in action ceases to exist, of course, it simply ceases to be rightly related to the Creator, and so, is no longer a divine mandate. Given the "dark

59. Ibid., 269–70 (italics original).

shadow" of the rebellious human being that infiltrates all the mandates, one might conclude that such a failure rightly to fulfill God's intention within the mandate would hardly be an aberration or cause for wonder. On the contrary, one might rightly expect such to be the rule, rather than the exception. Given people's penchant for finding an exception clause to provide the necessary latitude that justifies a preferred thought or course of action (a penchant displayed with particular passion in the arena of politics where people seem keen on discovering any excuse to validate their rejection of a government or government leader) however, it is important to recognize that Bonhoeffer actually moves in the opposite direction, and seeks to affirm the mandate as God's way of working—even when it might seem that in the particular instance under consideration, the time surely had come to reject such a lofty understanding.

The German theologian reminds his reader that whenever a mandate is accomplished by the responsible person or agency—even if it happens unconsciously or accidentally—then that party has a divine mandate. It is not necessary, for example, that a government openly acknowledge God or even acknowledge a responsibility to protect its citizens from harm. If that same government does, in fact, provide some semblance of security for the arenas of work and family, then that government is not to be judged as outside the bounds of the divine mandate. Bonhoeffer will have no part in fomenting sedition or even suspicion against the tangible examples of the mandates that people encounter in their everyday lives. Such a rebellious and cynical attitude would only serve to undermine the very thing he seeks to establish: the fundamental divinity and significance of each basic mandate. Given Bonhoeffer's own concrete situation in Nazi Germany, it is all the more remarkable that he is so guarded in granting the possibility of exceptions to the inherent divinity of any given instance of a mandate as encountered in life. While admitting the truth that some particular instance of work or family or government may, in fact, violate the Creator's will and intent, and so, forfeit its designation as a mandate; he does not urge or encourage his readers to assume or seek such deviations.

Even if there are failures on the part of those who are to shoulder the mandates, the mandates nevertheless prevail. Indeed, the divine mandate brings a certain dignity and purpose so that "what concretely exists receives relative justification through the divine mandate."[60] In other words, whether it is done grudgingly, distractedly, and badly or eagerly and earnestly, simply by the fact that the one carrying out a mandate is carrying out a mandate established by God, it has about it an aura of legitimacy and rightness. Bonhoeffer provides further caution against too quickly revoking the status of divine mandate to dubious creaturely action: "The existing marriage, government, etc., always has a relative advantage over what does not yet exist. Specific faults do not give the right to abolish or destroy what exists."[61] It is not hard to detect here another echo of Luther. When the reformer sought to bolster his theological argument against rebellion, he became utterly and typically pragmatic, warning his readers that rule by the mob is almost always much worse than rule by even a tyrant, let alone a bad prince.[62] Like Luther, Bonhoeffer was no anarchist, and not even much of a rebel—again, Bonhoeffer's antipathy to revolt casts his subsequent actions in opposition to the Third Reich in a yet more remarkable light.

Even when a particular human agency responsible for the pursuit of a mandate does actually utterly fail, and the divine mandate is forfeited, Bonhoeffer continues to resist any endorsement of rejection and revolution, but instead, urges return and restoration. When a concrete instance of a mandate falls short of the divine ordering and purpose, and so, risks losing its status as a mandate, the failure is not justification for rejection of that particular expression of the mandate. These specific failures "rather prompt a return to a true ordering under [Unterordnung] the divine mandate, and a restoration of true responsibility for the divine task."[63] The goal is to bring the existing

---

60. Ibid., 70.
61. Ibid.
62. *LW* 45, 62–63.

keeper of the mandate into conformity with the Creator's will and purpose. The one who rightly fulfills the mandate lives in submission to the Creator's direction. "Such true responsibility," Bonhoeffer explains, "consists in aligning the concrete form of the divine mandates with their origin, existence, and their goal in Jesus Christ."[64] While he does not in this place elaborate on who exactly would do the restoring of whatever concrete form was failing, it is clear from other passages in his *Ethics* that the other faithful concrete forms or keepers of the mandates rightly would shoulder this burden. Of course, this is precisely the line of thought evident throughout Luther's explication of the Psalm considered in chapter 1. Should a government leader falter or fail in the conduct of his mandate, then the church—or more specifically, its appointed leader and spokesman—may appropriately call that leader to repentance and guide him to restoration within his mandate. Conversely, should the church neglect its peculiar task, it is conceivable, at least to Luther, that a faithful keeper of the mandate given to the state could intervene and help to return the church to its proper place. In this way, God's provision for his creation through the mandates is honored and followed. Thus, the stewardship of God's creation according to God's plan for the good of God's people seems to be precisely the driving concern for Bonhoeffer, even as it was for Luther.

Conclusion

As with any tenet of orthodox teaching, care must be taken rightly to understand and use Luther's distinction between the two realms of God's activity in this world. Too easily, the distinction can degenerate into a divorce that leaves God's reality and the Christian person bifurcated. Potential liabilities notwithstanding, however, Luther's teaching of the two realms, when presented and practiced in accord with the reformer's own example, should be appreciated as an expression of the church's teaching, in conformity with scripture and

63. Bonhoeffer, *Ethics*, 70.
64. Ibid.

with the *regula fidei*. As such, questions about the doctrine's relevance for the contemporary world or direct challenges against its continued practice are essentially ruled out. To resist or reject the teaching would be to war against God's revealed truth. The work of Dietrich Bonhoeffer substantiates this view as it illustrates the timelessness of Luther's teaching as well as the dynamic way the teaching addresses a world quite unlike the world of Luther. Even as Bonhoeffer was able to follow the reformer's guidance on the interface of the spiritual and temporal realms and provide fresh teaching for his own context, so today, the Lutheran distinction between the two realms provides a viable and vibrant means of interpreting the surrounding world. The extent and force of Luther's dynamic will direct and animate the discussion of the next chapter which, it is hoped, will offer further evidence of the remarkable resource that Luther's thinking can provide not only for questions that directly concern the church and her theology but also for mundane and practical questions touching on the role of government, and more significantly, the responsibility of the church and her pastors in relation to the government. In this regard, each generation faces its own peculiar trials, of course, but such problems seem to abound and multiply with remarkable fecundity in the contemporary context.

4

Applying the Teaching to the Church and Her Pastors

Systematic theology endures a certain degree of opprobrium even from within the church.[1] And while it must be granted—albeit grudgingly—that some individual practitioners of the art of systematic theology certainly have contributed to its infamy, the larger problem stems from a perception that doctrine—which is, of course, the immediate purview of systematic theology—is largely irrelevant for "real life." Christians, whether those who occupy the pews or the pulpits, are primarily driven, it seems, by the desire for practical and applicable discussions and learning. In such a pragmatics-driven culture, a creeping disregard or even disdain for systematic theology is hardly surprising. Systematic theology is deemed too cerebral and perhaps even inherently scholastic. Again, I am well aware—from sometimes hard personal experience—that the stereotype is not

---

1. In the greeting line after one divine service in the first years of the new millennia, a retired clergyman, upon learning of my position in the department of systematic theology, unhesitatingly and unsmilingly opined: "There's nothing wrong in the church today that is not the fault of systematicians." The account is purely anecdotal, but quite representative, I think.

entirely unfounded or unjust. Nevertheless, the truth is that when rightly grasped, the very premise and definition of systematic theology should dispel all suggestions or suspicions of its irrelevance. Systematic theology is simply the contemporary application of God's timeless truth. In other words, systematic theology carefully considers and appraises the immediate context of the church and the world, and then, from the wealth of the church's deposit of truth, or its *regula fide*, it selects and speaks the appropriate aspect of God's truth for that culture. Indeed, if systematic theology is irrelevant, then it is not systematic theology. By definition, it must be both relevant and applicable to the immediate reality that surrounds it.

The truth of this claim is amply attested by the present discussion of the two realms. The teaching is grounded in the church's received tradition, the living content of the faith. It is doctrinally rich and profound as it describes the intricacies of God's work of creation, preservation, and his omnipotent rule over every aspect of the world. Yet, the teaching is eminently practical, guiding people to a better understanding of God's purposes and their individual roles within those purposes.[2] With the goal of concrete application firmly in view, it seems wise to begin with my own attempt at a clear, succinct, and yet comprehensive account of the two realms that is faithful to the teaching and practice of Luther.

The Two Realms Pattern and Guide

The teaching of the two realms—or more traditionally and familiarly, the two kingdoms—is not the idea of Martin Luther, or a creation of his immediate successors. It is an aspect of the church's deposit of faith, one part of the *regula fidei* that encompasses all the doctrinal content impacting both church and world as it relates and systematizes the narrative of God's activity in and for the world. Like any teaching, it can be misunderstood, twisted, and otherwise perverted into false and

2. For those interested in the historical evidence of this claim, John Witte provides an outstanding account of the early reformer's efforts to come to terms with the civil implications of their teaching. See John Witte Jr., *Law and Protestantism: The Legal Teachings of the Lutheran Reformation* (Cambridge: Cambridge University Press, 2002).

harmful caricatures of its true self, but as the dictum reminds us, abuse of a teaching does not negate the truth of the teaching. The structure and explanation offered here, then, is simply my effort accurately to capture and describe this doctrinal reality in a way beneficial to people living in the early years of the third Christian millennium. As with most facets of the Church's doctrine, the ideas are not complicated, and deceptively easy to state. God reigns over his creation, which has been infiltrated and distorted by the consequences of man's rebellious sin. According to his promise, God continues to unfold his plan to restore his creation and fulfill his original design for this world. God is at work in this broken world in two distinct ways, advancing his final purposes through both the temporal realm and the spiritual realm. Each realm has a peculiar sphere of responsibility and concern: the temporal realm most interested in the present, day-to-day affairs and interactions between the different creatures occupying God's world, and the spiritual realm focused on the relationship between creatures and the Creator and the ultimate fulfillment of this world's destiny at the eschatological consummation. Within these two realms, God provides institutions and leadership to accomplish his purposes and guides this process through his multifarious and dynamic revelation.

A simple chart below offers an overview and visual orientation of the balance and interrelationship between the two realms, and also provides a helpful guide for a brief discussion. First, it must be noted and appreciated that God is thoroughly in control of all that occurs in either the temporal or spiritual realms. The notion that the temporal realm somehow lies outside God's concern, or is, in some sense, unredeemed and the tool of Satan is utterly rejected. Thus, the temporal realm is correctly understood as under the "left-hand rule" of God and the spiritual under the "right-hand rule" of the same God. The left hand wields the sword of justice and the right offers the grace of the Word and Sacraments.

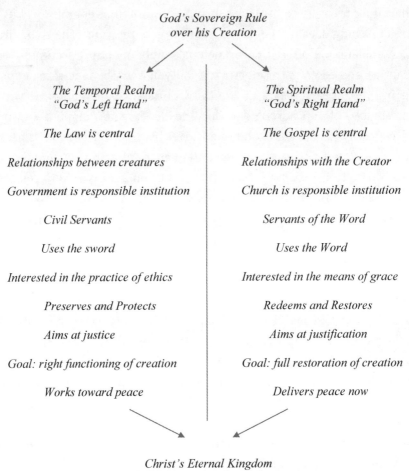

God's Sovereign Rule
over his Creation

The Temporal Realm	The Spiritual Realm
"God's Left Hand"	"God's Right Hand"
The Law is central	*The Gospel is central*
Relationships between creatures	*Relationships with the Creator*
Government is responsible institution	*Church is responsible institution*
Civil Servants	*Servants of the Word*
Uses the sword	*Uses the Word*
Interested in the practice of ethics	*Interested in the means of grace*
Preserves and Protects	*Redeems and Restores*
Aims at justice	*Aims at justification*
Goal: right functioning of creation	*Goal: full restoration of creation*
Works toward peace	*Delivers peace now*

Christ's Eternal Kingdom
Fully revealed at the Eschaton

Guiding axioms: *1. Distinction without Divorce*
                              2. Cooperation without Confusion

The two columns should be understood as comprehending the whole of creation—nothing lies beyond the scope of the two realms. Obviously, the descriptors aligned along each side of the chart are intended to be complementary and balancing. In the temporal realm, the law—that is, the will of God for his creation—is normative, while in the spiritual realm, everything is geared to the gospel's proclamation: the delivery of the forgiveness of sins through the life, death, and resurrection

within and according to God's overall plan for the reclamation and final restoration of his creation. On the last day, when that plan is fully consummated, the left-hand realm will not be obliterated and the right-hand realm acknowledged as the only true realm of God, after all; on that day, the state will not be wrapped into the church nor will the church be folded into the state. Rather, on that day, both state and church, and both temporal and spiritual realms with them, will be swept up together and fused again in the everlasting unity of Christ's unending glorious kingdom. Until that day, the spiritual and the temporal realms are indeed the two complementary hands of God working distinctively, yet in concert, to accomplish God's purposes for this world.

Understood in this way, the two realms teaching fosters an attitude and expectation toward both civil and ecclesial structures that is appropriate and realistic. Both realms seek to further God's agenda through institutions and leadership that is entirely human, and so, weak and broken. Consequently, it is quite possible that both leaders and structures in either realm may ignore or even reject the divine intention and operate in ways altogether self-serving or otherwise utterly corrupt. While the church easily recognizes this reality often painfully evident in the governments and authorities of the temporal realm; for its part, the state, most especially its spokesmen in the media, rarely has difficulty discovering embarrassingly human proclivities in the leaders and institutions of the spiritual realm. The doctrinal category of the two realms leads to a realism that finds neither situation particularly surprising or even necessarily problematic since the two realms understanding also provides reassurance that God will indeed accomplish his purpose through and even in spite of the machinations and perversions of leaders and institutions in both temporal and spiritual realms.

On the chart, a vertical line provides a visual demarcation between the two realms highlighting the importance of sharply distinguishing between the realms, along with the goals and methods peculiar to each. As the guiding axioms indicate, there must be a distinction that fends off any confusion between the realms. Nevertheless, from both scripture and Luther, it should be obvious that this line is, in fact, quite permeable, and perhaps better illustrated by a broken or dashed line. While each realm bears a unique responsibility designed and entrusted by God, they are not meant to operate in isolation from one another and certainly not in antagonism toward one another. Mutual harmony and concerted effort is the ideal. Of course, like even the most exemplary and encouraging relationship between genuinely loving siblings, a certain amount of tension, competition, and even conflict is hardly remarkable or a cause for much concern. So, as the guiding axioms indicate, the distinction between the two realms is not meant to create a divorce or lack of cooperation. In fact, when the two realms are operating as they should, each will encourage and exhort the other to do well what it has been given to do—and in the event of an absolute failure or obstinate refusal of one realm's guardians to fulfill their responsibility, the other realm's institutions and leaders may be compelled to intervene and seek to restore the right functioning of the floundering realm.[4] Naturally, the specific applications of this truth can pose some knotty challenges and create some lively discussion with final conclusions that are far from unanimous, but the basic idea is clear enough.

Before leaving the imagery and direction provided by the chart, one last clarifying point should be added. Between the two vertical columns of corresponding traits, one may sketch a saintly stickman to represent the Christian believer (a halo or a lapel cross might be a nice choice as a symbol adequate for the purpose). The message conveyed by the addition of the sanctified stick figure is at once simple and significant: the Christian believer lives simultaneously in both realms, concurrently benefitting from the gifts of each realm and fulfilling specific responsibilities within and for each realm. Sometimes, the

4. This understanding sheds bright light on Luther's appeal to the "Christian Nobility of the German Nation" to insert themselves directly into efforts to reform the church (LW 44, 123–217). Luther's enlistment of civil rulers to further the cause of the spiritual realm frankly baffles and embarrasses a vast array of theologians of all stripes. But, when seen through the lens of the two realms as presented here, it not only makes complete sense, but is recognized as altogether faithful to Christian doctrine.

114

Christian may be facing—and so, more fully focused on—one realm or the other, but the believer does not so much move between the realms as inhabits both at once. No doubt, in the course of living before both his Creator and his fellow creatures, the Christian will take stock of which relationship is in view and respond accordingly—now relishing the gift of the gospel in the spiritual realm, and then later, delighting to live in obedience to the law in the temporal realm. Such an approach to life produces not a wooden bifurcation of duties or thinking, much less a schizophrenic rending of the person, but actually produces a believer who knows and celebrates what it means to be a creature living as he was created to live before both God and creation.[5]

Be the Church

Following Luther and thinking clearly about God's two-handed care of his fallen creation yields great clarity in understanding the work peculiar to each realm, and also helps institutions and individuals doing the work to focus sharply on those tasks unique to their realm even as they appreciate and support the work being done in the complementary realm. Churches do not marshal military forces, and governments do not celebrate the Eucharist—that much should be indisputable. Still, at the same time, as argued above, the particular emphasis and focus of each realm does not preclude interaction between the realms or even the possibility of one realm venturing to support or even accomplish the work of the other in a case of extreme need. Of course, this is where things become interesting and even confounding. Indeed, lest the teaching outlined here be deemed an academic exercise only, and so, too easily dismissed as simplistic or unhelpful, it is time to practice the doctrine, apply the paradigm, and consider some of the concrete realities that confront both churches and Christians seeking to live faithfully in the world.

Above all, one must recognize the distinctive and definitive role of

---

5. With special thanks to Rev. Matthew Richardt who served as guest presenter during an early iteration of the seminary course, "Civil Affairs," and through his insight and experiences gained as a navy chaplain not only enhanced the leaning of my students but helped me develop and sharpen the concepts and terminology expressed in the chart.

the church in God's plan for the world. The unique identity and burden of the church is to be the presence and the proclaimer of the gospel in the fallen creation. There is no other institution in all of creation charged with the task of making known and offering the forgiveness and restoration accomplished by Jesus for the sake of this world. The church must be the place that delivers the gospel. Whatever else the church may choose to do for the sake of God's creation—and, as will be made clear as my argument progresses, it may do many things for the temporal good of the surrounding creation—it must never forsake its singular and determinative work. It must always be the place that announces and delivers God's perfect grace in Christ. When the church becomes distracted by temporal concerns or preoccupied with goals and purposes properly within the purview of the left-hand realm, the gospel is neglected, and in time, will be forsaken. Thus, the clear and careful distinction between the two realms is driven by a commitment to the gospel and its potent proclamation. For the sake of the gospel, the realms must be distinguished.

When the church is simply being the church, gathering to hear and learn God's Word, celebrating God's grace given at the font, honoring Christ's last testament in the receiving of his body and blood, giving and receiving forgiveness, forming and encouraging its own people into a life of discipleship lived in conformity with the Holy Spirit's purposes, and caring for the physical, emotional, and spiritual needs of those in and around the church, the church is doing precisely what God calls it to do.[6] In these actions, in this way of being in the world, the church is a living proclamation of the gospel's truth and is fulfilling what God calls it to do in and for the world. Indeed, as God has designed and arranged it, when the church follows the sort of distinctive practices that define it as briefly outlined above, then it not only fulfills God's intentions for her right functioning, but it also serves the world

---

6. Of course, as one might expect, this description of the church being the church corresponds smoothly with the marks of the church that Luther variously enumerates, but whose lists always include Word and sacrament, and usually Christian encouragement (discipline). See his extended discussion in his essay "On the Councils and the Church" from 1539 (LW 41, 148–66) in which he enumerates seven marks of the church: preaching, Baptism, the Lord's Supper, church discipline, the pastoral office, worship, and the cross of suffering.

around—the world of the temporal realm—by virtue of the church's very "otherness" centered on and celebrating the gospel. The world will see the church being the church in her distinctive worship and in the lives lived by her people, and doing such things with determination and deliberation. Seeing this, the world witnesses God's redemptive work in action, hears the call to know and follow God's purposes, is reminded of the penultimate nature of its own work and objectives, and is encouraged better to accomplish its given tasks for the sake of the created world.

Though he almost certainly intended an emphasis and "community" different than the one that would form around the thoughts advanced in this book, I believe that the idea of the church's service to the world that I am trying to outline does capture the sense of Stanley Hauerwas' oft-cited quote: "The church does not have a social ethic; the church is a social ethic."[7] Indeed, though he is certainly not an advocate for Luther's thinking in terms of two realms, Hauerwas frequently makes arguments about the church's identity and purpose that support my claim about the church's most important service to the world:

> The primary social task of the church is to be itself—that is, a people who have been formed by a story that provides them with the skills for negotiating the danger of this existence, trusting in God's promise of redemption. . . . For the church to be, rather than have, a social ethic means we must recapture the social significance of common behavior, such as acts of kindness, friendship, and the formation of families.[8]

In other words, simply by being a faithful community or congregation of believers that gathers for worship and then guides individual Christians to live out the reality of God's truth, both law and gospel, in ordinary daily life and routine, the church makes its most important impact on the world.

Of course, for Hauerwas, a faithful Christian community by definition must be predicated on nonviolence—a requirement that

---

7. Stanley Hauerwas, *The Peaceable Kingdom: A Primer in Christian Ethics* (Notre Dame, IN: University of Notre Dame Press, 1983), 99.
8. Stanley Hauerwas, *A Community of Character: Toward a Constructive Christian Social Ethic* (Notre Dame, IN: University of Notre Dame Press, 1981), 10–11.

117

extends also to the individual Christian's engagement with the temporal realm and thereby categorically rejects any possibility of a believer wielding the temporal sword of justice for the sake of a neighbor in need. Following Luther and the teaching defended in previous chapters, I would, of course, counter that the reality of the Christian life compels one not only to deny self and forgo personal retaliation, but also to fulfill one's vocational responsibilities in the temporal realm, including, when necessary, bearing the sword as an arm of the state. I will return to this discussion and the importance of temporal vocations for the sake of the wider creation when I take up the impact of good two realms thinking on individual Christians. For now, I simply want to emphasize what Hauerwas argues: that by being the church unabashedly in practices of worship and community formation that are decidedly at odds with the assumptions and norms of the surrounding culture, and may be not only dismissed or disdained as "out of touch" but even denounced and attacked as inimical to modern society—that when the church functions like that, it is making its single greatest contribution to the temporal realm. Naturally, the truth of this reality may well be lost on the majority of those who populate the temporal realm. Still, the fact remains: when the church is faithful, the church is relevant, always.

Constantinianism

Much could be written on the phenomenon of Constantinianism; indeed, on this topic, much has been written, and certainly more is yet to be said. It is hardly my purpose here to leap into the midst of that often intricate and unwieldy discussion. However, I do believe that some pertinent reflections and immediate applications are in order as I seek to consider what it might mean for the church actually to embrace and rightly practice the paradigm of God's two realms. Constantinianism is the name given to the fourth-century rapprochement between the Christian church and the state, which at that time was, of course, the Roman Empire. Whatever the truth of Constantine's personal conversion and military gains under the shadow of the cross, or more accurately, behind chi rho-emblazoned shields, there is no doubt that he made great political gains from his tactical surrender to the Christian faith. More importantly, from the perspective of the church, his pragmatic decision to yield to the rising tide of Christianity in his realm signaled dramatic changes for the church. Whether on the whole, those were good changes or bad changes is part of the debate I would rather skirt at present. Whatever one's commitments to the legacy of Constantinianism, the label has become the standard term for an alliance between church and state that is considered by those in positions of authority to be mutually beneficial.[9] While the forms and manifestations have shifted through time, Constantinianism is still very much alive. Of course, Christians in the United States often assume some degree of exemption from the phenomenon of Constantinianism. After all, the country was founded on a commitment to the separation of church and state. One could reasonably assume a certain immunity to Constantinianism would result. But from the blue laws of previous decades to a de facto privileged position as the state religion, American Christianity has always operated in an environment saturated with the aroma of Constantinianism.

While it is certainly true that there has been a steady and seemingly systematic knocking away of the props once provided the church by the state, and it might appear that the demise of the alliance is imminent if not already accomplished, the reality of Constantinianism endures still today, especially in the greatest prop of all: the church's privilege of tax exempt status. It is this vestige of Constantinianism and its impact on the church that should foster at the very least a degree of skepticism about the purported advantages of Constantinianism. Indeed, regardless of what some might consider to be obvious benefits (freedom from the fear of torture and execution being perquisites even more significant, though too easily taken for granted, than freedom from taxation), the case can be made that in the way it is manifest in

---

9. An engaging, albeit negatively biased, introduction to the notion of Constantinianism and its significance for the church can be found in Stanley Hauerwas and William Willimon, *Resident Aliens: Life in the Christian Colony* (Nashville, TN: Abingdon, 1989), 15–48.

the contemporary Western context, Constantinianism must be labeled as a problem. Still, the thoughtful reader should recognize that this is not necessarily the case. In fact, one could use the axiom of "cooperation without confusion" to defend and legitimate the state choosing to award privileges and support to the church—including granting it an exemption from taxation. Such support could be considered an appropriate form of cooperation. When both realms of God's activity are functioning as they should, it is certainly at least theoretically conceivable that the church could receive aid or assistance from the government without compromising its identity or forsaking its work. Luther's own practice definitely reflects this conviction.

What might exist in theory, though, has proven difficult to produce in reality—at least in the reality of twenty-first-century America. In the present situation, the church's privilege of tax exempt status has shaped a church that too frequently fails in its work. It is an issue of systemic dependence and consequent acquiescence. Whether articulated or not, the fear of "losing tax exempt status" operates as a powerful factor underlying significant decisions made by parochial school administrators and teachers, church councils, denominational boards, pastors, and parishioners. The fear may be real or imaginary, but when Christians act or fail to act because they are fearful of forfeiting their church's tax-exempt privilege, then Constantinianism has effectively gagged the church's voice and stymied the church's work. There may be a variety of reasons, even very good or noble ones, for the state to grant tax-exempt status to the church, but when all is said and done, the policy amounts to a government handout in favor of the church.[10] But, the benefit is an illusion.

Dependence on the tax-exemption-handout does not serve, but damages the church. Unwilling to jeopardize its financial subsidy from

---

10. A congregation's youth leader dutifully presenting his carefully preserved "exemption letter" and saving his church $2.47 in sales tax for party supplies at the supermarket may seem inconsequential enough; but one can scarcely overestimate the institutional importance of exemption from the property tax on the 80 acres of suburban St. Louis that are home to Concordia Seminary where I teach.

the government, the church becomes cautious and compliant, holding back on speaking God's truth in all situations, hesitating to involve itself in anything that may be perceived as political; or the church may even become arrogant and defiant as it tries to preserve its privileged position and perquisites as if they were an inherent right. Neither position allows the church to function in the world and in relation to the world as it should. Cowed into silent and submissive dependence, the church does not deliver the clear and direct word of God to the world and its leaders and people with confidence and conviction. There is no "Thus saith the Lord!" The prophetic task is forsaken. Or, the church compromises its unique identity and work in the world as the proclaimer of the gospel of Jesus Christ and alienates and disgusts those who need to hear that news by presenting itself to the world as just one more special interest group jostling for an opening where it can insert its hungry snout at the public trough and fawning over power-brokers with its hand out. The church must never succumb to such groveling. Considering the current climate in the United States, it seems that the revocation of the church's tax-exempt status is simply a matter of time. Perhaps it is time now for the church to accept and even welcome this inevitability and start planning and acting accordingly. Indeed, a church faithful to its work would only serve to hasten the coming of that day—the contemporary Western world has little patience for those who will not abide its rules and expectations for appropriate behavior. And a church that declares the exclusivity of Christ's truth and the universality and permanence of God's moral law will certainly be deemed inappropriate in the enlightened culture of twenty-first-century America.

Of course, for many years now, the infection and corruption of Constantinianism have been recognized and there have been demands to curtail—if not eliminate—the unholy alliance. For the most part, the voices calling for an end to the cozy relationship have typically not come from within the church; indeed, such strident demands are usually considered a threat to the church. Rather, efforts to quash Constantinianism have most often been undertaken in defense of the state, and aim at creating a civil realm sanitized of all religious contamination. It is as if the noble state needs to be protected from the nefarious designs of the church! But, for Christians, it should be clear that the collusion of church and state that is Constantinianism must be rejected primarily not for the sake of the state, but for the sake of the church. When the church in America cowers under the outstretched hand of the state waiting for its beneficent provision, then the church cannot help but fail in its God-given tasks.

Patriotism in Church

Keeping with the present focus on the impact of good two realms thinking on the church community as a whole, and in light of my sharp criticism of Constantinianism, it is worth considering the church's expressions of patriotism. As so often in this discussion, we are faced again with a complicated situation. The church as an institution is part of the temporal realm and certainly benefits when that realm is functioning as it should: providing infrastructure and utilities; offering protection from crime, fire, and flood; and upholding justice. For these goods, the church should be grateful to both God and the leaders of the temporal realm. And the church should appropriately express this gratitude on a regular basis. Such gratitude may be voiced in the prayers of the church as well as in deliberate actions taken to thank and encourage civil servants. Indeed, the practice of habitually praying in the divine service for leaders by name is altogether good and right. Beyond this, the church, should not neglect opportunities to give expressions of thanks and gifts of gratitude to those who serve it in the civil realm: a special meal delivered to the fire station, notes of thanks and encouragement given to the police department, care boxes sent to those in the military, and a celebration of civil servants hosted at the church would all be fitting responses to the gifts given by the temporal realm.

Yet, while the church appreciates the state and concretely articulates that appreciation, it must not confound or confuse its own message by allowing patriotic gestures and practices to coopt its own unique identity and purpose. It is essential that the church remain the church—the proclaimer of God's gospel and the voice of God's moral code spoken to the world for the world's own sake, both its guidance and its repentance. With that in mind, there are certain practices, otherwise good and wholesome even for believers, that do not belong within the life and especially the worship of the church. The church delivers the gospel, pointing people to the great and universal reality of the fatherhood of God and of the grace poured out through Christ. The church should be wary of practices or actions that are peculiarly limited to one nation or people group, and should deliberately and pointedly reject activities or rites within the church's worship that explicitly celebrate and promote the institutions and practices of the temporal realm rather than the spiritual realm. Such expressions within the church's worship life should be recognized for what they are: vestiges of Constantinianism. The very real threat is that the clear message of the gospel will be compromised and even forfeited by the confusion of the realms fostered by practices of patriotism in conjunction with the church's worship.

It seems that some specificity is in order here, lest the reader speculate and reach conclusions quite at variance with my intentions. To be specific, pledging one's allegiance to the American flag is well and good at the outset of a school day or before a meeting of the local town council, but it has no place within the divine service. Singing the "Star Spangled Banner" with a patriotic crowd can be a wonderful experience at the ballpark, but is altogether out of place in the congregation's sanctuary. And while the nation's flag may fly along the church's street side frontage where it can be seen by every passing vehicle, it has no place behind the altar or in the chancel. Gratitude for the nation can be expressed and veterans honored in ways much more fitting and significant than displaying a country's flag in the sacred space of the church. Besides, the days of needing to find some way to demonstrate the depth of the church's loyalty to America against charges of sympathy for a foreign—especially German—enemy are long past. The nation's flag is an intruder in the church's sanctuary. Neither is it sufficient to "balance" the US flag with a contrived "Christian flag" conjured with all the creativity and artistic imagination a nineteenth-century Sunday school volunteer could muster. Rich with symbols and images far more profound than the heraldry of nations, the church needs no flag. Indeed, the crucifix and the creed are in no way enhanced when supplemented with a Christian flag complete with its own clumsy, manufactured pledge.

The sanctuary is the designated space of God's particular presence in this world. It is here that his Word is proclaimed. Here, his forgiveness is declared. Here, children are baptized into the kingdom. Here, God's grace is placed into the mouths of his people. This space is the unique place where spiritual realities are delivered and celebrated. This is the church's space. This is God's space. It is the space of the spiritual realm, the vertical dimension of existence focused on God's gospel. Symbols of the left-hand temporal realm simply do not belong here. Is the church's confession somehow tied to the American system of government? Is the church's purpose allied with the goals and objectives of the United States? Are the church's people synonymous with the population of the country? Is the church's existence bound to the rise and fall of the state? The church and her confession are of a different nature altogether than those of the state, and conflating the two in the divine service or in the chancel's adornment does not advance patriotism. Instead, it leads the church to confuse people both inside and outside the church, it blunts the church's distinctive message, and it obscures and ultimately obliterates the gospel. There is a line that must separate cooperation from confusion, and that line must be carefully observed, especially in the worship life of the church.

Politics in the Pulpit

A sharp demarcation between the realms, as argued above, should not however, be oversimplified and trivialized into a single-minded and unthinking rule that forbids all "politics" in the church. Excluding flags and patriotic ritual from the church's chancel and worship does not mean excluding politics from the worship life of the church. Obviously, this position may well seem more than a little inconsistent. It is, however, entirely in line with the teaching of the two realms. Patriotic expressions would violate the axiom against causing confusion of the realms, but forbidding all politics would ignore the axiom warning against a divorce between the realms. Considered from the most basic approach, it is obvious that a faithful pastor must address questions of a political nature from the pulpit. It is, after all, a pastor's responsibility to preach to the real life situations, circumstances, questions, struggles, and needs of his congregation. Family issues, financial concerns, work and leisure struggles, questions about morality, spirituality, and guilt before God and neighbor are all unhesitatingly recognized as aspects of relevant preaching. Yet, how significant and pressing to the members of a congregation are questions and issues that are altogether political? Does it matter to the people sitting in the pews who wins the next election, whether Congress passes a new immigration law, or how the supreme court settles questions about abortion, euthanasia, or the definition of marriage? Obviously, these are issues almost always relevant to a sizable number of parishioners, and at times, issues that press very hard on virtually all who gather for worship—only those too young to care would find the topic irrelevant. Some may find the topic uncomfortable, and a few might find it offensive, but none will find it irrelevant! The truth is that the politics of the temporal realm matter to people, and they matter to God. Thus, a church and her faithful pastor cannot ignore what is political simply because it is political and might generate some discomfort. To discharge his office faithfully, it is imperative that the pastor deliberately and carefully provide the congregation guidance in how rightly to think and act when it comes to questions that are political.

It should be evident that taking up topics of a political nature, whether in the pulpit or in a Bible class, will always account for a small fractional part of the overall content of the church's preaching and teaching. Timely and relevant preaching that touches on what is overtly political must appear as only of secondary or even tertiary importance as a topic for discussion and reflection in the church. But when appropriate, it will—indeed, it must—be a topic for the church to consider. Political questions matter to people, and God and his church do have something to say to God's people about political questions. It is a great mistake for the church to take a stance of silence on issues such as abortion, immigration, military intervention, euthanasia, or even taxation simply because these are political topics. They are all topics that matter to people, and they are all topics that matter to God. What God has to say must be said, and it must be said to his people in particular; it is the business of the pastor, and it is a topic worthy of the pulpit. Naturally, the specifics of such preaching vary far too widely by time and place for any attempt at precise direction here. Always, though, what is critical is that God's truth about a topic is delivered so that people can be formed into thinking rightly about that and related topics. This is not a time for a pastor to express personal sentiment or opinion—actually, it is questionable whether there ever exists a time in the pulpit when such a course is in order. Rather, the faithful pastor speaks confidently about God's wisdom and God's direction for the right functioning of this world and does not hesitate to point out when these things are threatened or violated by government action, inaction, policy, or legislation. For example, a pastor not only could, but absolutely should, have something to say about a legislative body working to legalize and regulate prostitution. It is vital that the church has the ability, and better yet, that it develop the habit, of being able to speak plainly and confidently to such temporal realm, political issues. The very practice of addressing such issues from the pulpit is significant for the formation of the congregation. The people are led better to understand and appreciate God's rule over all the earth and the church's responsibility to speak God's truth into that world. They are encouraged to see all of their lives—including the political aspect of their lives in the context of God's encompassing word and will. Indeed, whether or not the wider public notices or cares what the church has to say to it may not be as significant as the impact that such speaking will certainly have on the church's own membership.

If the church chooses not to speak, what is certain is that the people of the church, and the wider world that may or may not listen, will be left only with the massive and persuasive input that floods over them in unrelenting waves from the world's capable spokesmen eager to shape their thoughts and actions. To counteract the tide of errant and evil thinking that washes through all the various media outlets, the church must boldly declare God's way of thinking about particular questions besetting the temporal realm. It needs to talk about politics, so that people can hear what God has to say about such things. Does this mean that the pastor will tell people how to vote? Well, yes, in some sense, he might do exactly that. Before dismissing this idea as an intolerable violation of individual autonomy and a repudiation of all that is sacred in America, consider the possibility of a referendum to legalize pederasty—would not the church's unequivocal teaching about such things amount to telling a parishioner how to vote? And is the church's audacity to instruct a person how to vote any more intrusive or overweening than the church telling that same person with whom she can have sex, or how she should spend her Sunday mornings? Learning to listen to God's truth and direction takes practice, and may, at times, be both unfamiliar and uncomfortable, but those in the church need to listen, and those charged with delivering that truth need to speak—whether that truth impacts a person's sex life or political life.

What is said from the pulpit will, though, always be limited to and guided by what is actually clearly taught within the church's deposit of faith. That is to say, the pastor will speak with authority on a topic only when scripture and the church speak with authority on that topic. By necessity, the political questions or problems addressed from the pulpit will always be of a compelling moral nature. Issues lacking a clear moral component will also lack an authoritative word from the church's deposit of faith, and so, would lie beyond the pastor's concern. Obviously, there is a great deal in the world of politics that would not and should not be addressed from the pulpit. Pastors are called to declare the whole counsel of God to the world, and must do that with courage and conviction. But when God's counsel is silent, so must they be. In other words, while a pastor should speak out against violations of God's revealed will for the right functioning of his creation, the pastor should not venture to offer direction for the specifics of exactly how an elected official should govern. His task is not to instruct government leaders and civil servants about the particular way they should solve this or that problem. Following Luther's wise counsel, the pastor does not venture into the particulars involved in fulfilling any given task of the temporal realm.[11] A pastor does not tell a city council how to combat crime, a Congress how to fight a just war, or a mayor how to pay for a new bridge. Still, that same pastor can certainly challenge and call to repentance any of those three when their actions—even actions taken in the course of fulfilling their office—violate a clear word from God. As seen in Luther's treatment of Psalm 82 covered in chapter 1, it is quite right and even necessary for a pastor to address the shortcomings of a civil ruler, and to do it in public from the pulpit.

All this being said, it bears repeating once more: the pastor's first and driving task is to preach Christ and the gospel of forgiveness of sins. This is his call. Yet, within the ongoing life of the congregation, and in an effort to speak to the problems and situations of his flock, he will also, always, address any number of topics included beneath the heading: the law, or the will of God for his creation. It is inevitable, in the course of such preaching, that political topics will, from time to time, present themselves as topics of pressing concern—and when they do, the pastor can and should take the occasion to address them.

Out into the World

When the pastor is preaching from his own pulpit, he can and should preach with confidence whatever his people need to hear on whatever pressing topic confronts them in world or in text. But what should the pastor say when he is not in the familiar and presumably friendly

---

11. *LW* 46, 266–67. In this instance Luther is warning against entering into the fray over questions about engagements and subsequent marriages. His argument against giving specific advice is simple: it is not his business. Yet, it is important to note that after his warning against such action, he actually relents to the repeated requests of those in the temporal realm and does offer concrete and specific counsel!

environment of his own pulpit, chancel, and parishioners? What should he say when he ventures beyond the clear but permeable boundary of the spiritual realm and steps into the temporal realm? Specifically, what should the pastor say on those singular occasions when he is asked to serve a particular function for the sake of the other realm with its sword, soldiers, and statesmen? If negotiating the interface between the spiritual and the temporal realms is akin to sailing through shallow waters laced with reefs, then considering the possibility of a pastor stepping into an event of the temporal realm in his role as pastor is attempting to sail the same waters at night in a storm.[12] Along with the problems of distinguishing the two realms, one must also consider the very real possibility of becoming, wittingly or not, embroiled in activities that smack of unionism and even syncretism. In this light, determining whether any given event should be classified as worship or as merely a secular gathering becomes a vital question, followed closely by the need to establish the identities and affiliations of those who will participate, and to what degree, in some aspect of conducting the event. Of course, undergirding and defining this problem is the tension that rightly exists between the worthy urge to seize any opportunity to speak God's truth to those who may not otherwise hear, over against the desire not to compromise that same truth by giving an impression that differences of doctrine and practice among Christians are of no significance.

These are all serious concerns, touching on significant questions about gospel witness, Christian unity, and clarity of confession. They should not be ignored; nevertheless, a full and careful consideration of such important issues lies well beyond the scope of the present discussion. While much more could be said, and I would not mind saying it, at present, I shall content myself with two assertions, or maxims: those who consider the answers to such questions to be

---

12. A skeptic only needs to consider the CTCR document on "Guidelines for Participation in Civic Events" published in 2004 to appreciate the astounding array and complexity of the issues involved with such an enterprise—and the rancor such an undertaking can arouse. One could hardly consider it surprising were an enlightenment-seeking reader to suggest that the document is more successful at generating questions and confusion than at answering and dispelling them.

"simple" or "obvious" certainly have failed to give sufficient deliberation to the breadth and depth of the issues involved. Questions touching on witness, fellowship, and confession are inherently complex and confounding, and it seems that virtually every scenario comes with its own peculiar "extenuating circumstances" that prevent it from fitting neatly into a predetermined paradigm or solution. In this discussion, there seem to be few answers that are uncontestable givens or always-applicable axioms. Thus, the need for my second maxim: charity and respect must be extended to brothers in the ministry who are confronted with invitations and situations that demand immediate answers—even when one may not agree with the answer reached and actions taken. But as I said, pursuing a complete and compelling consideration of these questions is not the task at hand. It is enough for now to address the two most basic questions: Should a pastor speak at an event that is overwhelmingly temporal or secular in nature, and if so, what should he say?

It might seem that while finding an answer to the first question could generate some discussion, the answer to the second should engender little or no debate—indeed, it should be a foregone conclusion. I disagree. Given the paradigm of the two realms, I think that an answer to the first question is relatively easily reached—but a thoughtful answer to the second question may well provoke some interesting and contentious differences of opinion. To bring clarity to this discussion, a hypothetical situation will provide a concrete point of departure; and to avoid the maddening complexity noted in the previous paragraphs and focus on the task at hand, I shall create an "ideal" scenario free of complicating factors. My imaginary pastor serves a parish in a small Midwestern city where, with some regularity, he participates in the monthly meetings of the local ministerial alliance. According to a rotating schedule and local custom, he is invited by the city council to attend their next regular business meeting and offer a "prayer of blessing" at the beginning of the proceedings. No direction and no restrictions regarding the prayer's content are prescribed. The pastor has full latitude to pray as he chooses. So, what does he choose? I believe that a solid understanding of the two realms would prompt the pastor to accept the invitation without hesitation. This is not a worship service, there are no other clergy present. The event is wholly and safely secular and free of any syncretistic or unionistic overtones. It is simply an opportunity for the pastor to communicate his affirmation and support of the local government and its leaders. Further, it is a chance, in some small way, to cultivate a relationship of mutual support between the two realms of God's provision for his creation. There is no compelling theological reason to decline the invitation.

The pastor should go to the meeting and offer a prayer. But what should he say; what should he include in his prayer? Conventional counsel would be to offer a Trinitarian prayer seeking guidance for the leaders and accentuating the uniquely Christian proclamation of the gospel of Jesus Christ. This approach would interpret the event almost exclusively through the lens of the spiritual or right-hand realm. Simply put, the prayer would be seen as an opportunity to preach Christ to those who need to hear. Fair enough; it would not be difficult to build a compelling case in support of this approach. But what if this city-council-prayer opportunity was viewed not from the perspective of the spiritual realm, but from the vantage of the temporal, left-hand realm? What if the pastor interpreted this chance to pray not primarily as an open door to do evangelism, but as a chance to support and advance the work of the temporal realm? If the compelling concern is the right functioning of the temporal realm, then the pastor would understand his visit to the meeting as a foray into the left-hand realm, where he would accept and affirm the objectives and purposes of that realm. Considered from this viewpoint, the prayer might contain rather a different content. The pressing task, then, would be to remind the members of the council of the divine grounding of their task, the overriding goal of justice that should drive them in their work, and their accountability to the Creator as they discharge their responsibilities. In other words, his message will be law, not gospel;

and in light of a clear understanding of God's two realms, I believe that this course is not only defensible, but preferable.

Pastors trained to serve within the spiritual realm can be forgiven for bristling at the notion that they would ever intentionally craft a message that did not aim at proclaiming Christ with clarity and conviction.[13] Still, the idea of ending a message (in whatever form it takes: prayer, invocation, blessing, or address) with the law is defensible not only within the doctrinal parameters of the two realms but also from the most basic distinction between law and gospel. It bears remembering that no less an authority on preaching law and gospel than C. F. W. Walther made the point about the role of the law rather emphatically. Commenting on Christ's admonition not to cast pearls before swine, the great churchman declared:

> What is meant by "pearls"? The consolation of the Gospel, with the grace, righteousness, and salvation which it proclaims. Of these things we are not to speak to dogs, that is, to enemies of the Gospel; nor to swine, that is, to such as want to remain in their sins and are seeking their heaven and their bliss in then filth of their sins.[14]

As his argument progressed, Walther sharpened his words:

> Accordingly, we may not preach the Gospel, but must preach the Law to secure sinners. . . . Unless the rocky subsoil in their hearts has been pulverized by the Law, the sweet Gospel is of no benefit to them. . . . If remission of sins without repentance is preached, the people imagine that they have already forgiveness of sins, and thereby they are made secure and unconcerned. *This is a greater error and sin than all errors of former times.*[15]

---

13. Of course, praying and preaching are not the same thing. The objective of a prayer of intercession is typically not the same as that of preaching. However, I would aver that in my scenario, and in most situations when a pastor is invited by the temporal realm to serve that realm in some formal capacity, regardless of how the desired words or activities are designated or described, the pastor should treat them in essentially the same way: as opportunities to speak God's truth to those who are present. Even a prayer becomes a "message."

14. C. F. W. Walther, *The Proper Distinction between Law and Gospel: Thirty-Nine Evening Lectures*, trans. W. H. T. Dau (St. Louis, MO: Concordia, 1928), 114.

15. Ibid., 118, 119, 123 (italics in original).

No repentance, no gospel. So a message that focuses on delivering the law to those who need to repent is consistent with a proper distinction between law and gospel.

The law can be preached to stir hearts to repentance, or to instill in those hearts a desire to "do the right thing" (whether the primary motive driving that desire is fear, obligation, gratitude, or love matters little in the temporal realm). Either way, the content of the law is the same: the will of God for the way that his creation is designed to function. It is the same law that curbs and impels behavior and that unmasks sin and failure. The pastor, then, becomes the messenger of that law to the temporal realm. The critical thing is not only to recognize but also to appreciate the fact that the temporal realm with its focus on justice and upholding God's law is its own legitimate end. When it fulfills its responsibilities, it does God's work. Thus, a pastor can, at times, join in that good and godly work for its own sake. He can assert the law of God, call officials to conform to that law, urge the cause of justice, and knowingly refrain from speaking the gospel of grace and justification in that situation. When the goal is to support the work of the temporal realm, the last word in that context is the law. Of course, when the goal is the full and final restoration of the entire creation and the complete healing of the relationship between creature and Creator, and creature and all other creatures, the last word is always the gospel. So, the pastor needs to know in which realm he serves at any given moment, and the goal appropriate to each situation.

The Degree of Revelation Principle

It is, as I already noted, critical to accept and value the fact that the left-hand temporal realm is God's realm. The structure, the objectives, the guiding law are all from God, and those who carry out work within and for the sake of this realm are doing God's work. The pastor who comes alongside these civil servants to encourage, aid, exhort, praise, or upbraid them as appropriate is serving God by helping these servants serve more capably and faithfully—that is, more in line with

God's purposes. It may be helpful to employ what I refer to as the "degree of revelation principle" when sorting out the best way to proceed in any given situation. The principle is simple: speak about God to the extent that he has made himself known in the place where you are speaking. When addressing a gathering in the civil realm, God has certainly made himself known. As St. Paul reminds us, God's law is at work in the creation itself pricking and soothing consciences, and providing the parameters and structure that guide all of life in the world. So, whether known by name or not, God is certainly known in the civil realm. The pastor who steps into that realm talks about God in those terms. He speaks about God's sovereign rule as Creator. He talks about God's perfect will. He declares the standard of justice and upholds the value of every part of creation, and especially, the priceless worth of each human creature. But in that realm, the full gospel has not been revealed. The gospel belongs to the spiritual realm. The gospel reigns without rival in the right-hand realm. When the pastor addresses those gathered in the spiritual realm, he savors the privilege of speaking the full revelation of God and proclaims the gospel of full forgiveness in Christ. In the civil realm, in the halls of justice, the pastor declares the law of the God who rules and judges his creation; in the church, in the divine service, he trumpets the gospel of the God who loves and dies for his creation. He speaks in each venue about God to the extent that God has made himself known. He follows the degree of revelation principle.

It is worth noting that the approach I am advocating not only aligns with, but honors, the clear and direct counsel Luther provides in his Great Galatians Commentary of 1535. Supplying extensive instruction on the need to hold sharp distinctions between several of the fundamental dualities in the Christian faith, Luther brings together the binary tensions of law and gospel, the two kinds of righteousness, and the two realms—all of which are, of course, intimately related when in action. There is value, as there always is, in letting Luther speak at some length:

In society, on the other hand, obedience to the Law must be strictly required. There let nothing be known about the Gospel, conscience, grace, the forgiveness of sins, heavenly righteousness, or Christ Himself; but let there be knowledge only of Moses, of the Law and its works. When these two topics, the Law and the Gospel, are separated this way, both will remain within their limits. The Law will remain outside heaven, that is, outside the heart and the conscience; and, on the other hand, the freedom of the Gospel will remain outside the earth, that is outside the body and its members. And just as soon as the Law and sin come into heaven, that is, into the conscience, they should be promptly ejected. For then the conscience should know nothing about the Law and sin but should know only about Christ. On the other hand, when grace and freedom come into the earth, that is, into the body, you must say: "You have no business here among the dirt and filth of this physical life. You belong in heaven!" . . . In a matter apart from conscience, when outward duties must be performed, then, whether you are a preacher, a magistrate, a husband, a teacher, a pupil, etc., this is no time to listen to the Gospel. You must listen to the Law and follow your vocation.[16]

It is obvious that Luther fully appreciated the legitimacy and importance of the temporal realm, and knew with certainty that in that realm, the law alone was the normative word. Obviously, Luther was also well aware of the absolutely vital importance of the gospel. Yet, he was able to recognize and urge appropriate limits on its proclamation and exercise. The temporal realm, as Luther saw it, was no place for the gospel! Shocking as this may sound at first, it is completely in accord with his teaching on the two realms. So it is that the degree of revelation principle, or the counsel to speak in the civil realm about the law without presenting the gospel, is also quite consistent with a right understanding of the two realms.

It should be apparent that I am absolutely advocating the idea that a pastor may faithfully discharge his responsibility toward the civil realm by speaking to that realm only about the God who created, watches, and finally judges those who live and serve in the temporal world. I am not, however, suggesting that the pastor forsake the gospel. Rather, the pastor treasures both law and gospel and maintains a perspective wide enough to see both realms of God's activity in the

16. *LW* 26, 116, 117.

world, and the determinative word of God for each. He realizes that by preaching the law faithfully and forcefully, he will inevitably drive residents of the temporal realm to a realization of their need for some relief from the inevitable burden of the law—and when declared well, the law will always present such a burden. Those who hear the pastor's clarion declaration of God's law would recognize that pastor as a person to be trusted to speak God's word without compromise or apology, and when smitten by the unendurable weight of the law, might well seek his further aid and counsel. Of course, once those convicted by the law enter the spiritual realm—in whatever setting that might occur—the pastor would seize the opportunity to proclaim to them the gospel in all its life-giving potency and specificity. Such is the dynamic of law and gospel as applied in the two realms.

A few tangential observations are in order before tying up this cursory consideration of the pastor's role in serving at civic events. It is a standard position that no pastor can abide a restriction on his delivery of a "message" in the civil realm that would prevent him from explicit mention of the Trinity or Christ. As noted in the CTCR document addressing civic events:

> Offering prayers, speaking, and reading Scripture at events sponsored by governments, public schools and volunteer organizations would be a problem if the organization in charge restricted a Christian witness. For instance, if an invitation requires a pastor to pray to God without mentioning Jesus, he cannot in good conscience accept.[17]

I disagree. In light of a right understanding of the two realms, and employing the degree of revelation principle, I believe that a pastor could speak of God only according to his law, as he has revealed himself as Creator and Judge, without the need to invoke further truths of Christian confession.[18] This is not a rejection of God's full truth, but

---

17. CTCR, "Guidelines for Participation in Civic Events" (LCMS, 2004), 3.
18. While I do not intend to imply that he necessarily endorses or supports the position presented here, William Schumacher at least argues in a similar direction in a 2004 essay. He writes, "an acknowledgement of God by government or civic leaders serves as a crucial and meaningful reminder of the penultimate nature of the authority of the state. This is the case with the inclusion of the motto 'In God we trust' on the coins and currency of the United States. Such a motto is religiously generic and unspecified, and thus theologically inadequate. But the usefulness

a wise use of that truth in the appropriate situation. Obviously, discernment and caution are in order as the pastor determines the possibility of participating with such restrictions. A pastor might well conclude that he cannot accept such limitations. Such a decision would be quite understandable and should be supported by other pastors. However, another pastor who concludes that the situation warrants a clear speaking of God's law, and who agrees to the restrictions, should not be deemed as a traitor to his confession or a denier of his Lord. He should expect not only questions and requests for clarification, but also finally the support of other pastors.

Finally, it should be recognized that the temporal realm interactions of the Apostle Paul are not exactly applicable to the present discussion. When Paul preached in the temporal realm, he preached! In other words, he was doing right-hand, spiritual realm work, calling people to repent and to receive God's re-creating gift of the gospel. He was not cooperating with the temporal realm or supporting the servants of that realm in their particular calling. The contemporary parallel of Paul's address in Athens, for example, would not be a prayer at a city council meeting, but an evangelistic/apologetic conversation with a group of skeptical college students. And while Paul's defense before Felix and Festus is not an example of what to say in a civic event; it would provide exceptional guidance for a pastor who one day faces legal charges for his preaching of God's truth. In the culture in which Paul lived and worked, the very notion of his receiving an invitation to offer a prayer or message at some civic occasion is comically absurd. Paul did not employ the degree of revelation principle because it was irrelevant for him. Paul simply never had the chance to consider whether to accept an invitation to provide a prayer for a civic event, or what to say if he consented. In our contemporary context, however, at least

of such an acknowledgement does not depend on a theologically precise definition of the referent (God). Rather such references are extremely important because they express a fundamental self-limitation of government, and the recognition that there is a transcendent divine power to which citizens, and even the sovereign state itself, are subject and accountable" (William Schumacher, "Civic Participation by Churches and Pastors: An Essay on Two Kinds of Righteousness," *Concordia Journal* 30, no. 3 [July, 2004]: 174–75). The point, as I see it, is that while a generic reference to God is insufficient for the full account of God required in a presentation of God's gospel story, that "thin" or truncated reference is quite adequate for the purposes of the temporal realm.

for now and for a while longer perhaps, such opportunities do still occasionally present themselves to pastors.[19] The wise pastor will consider such invitations from all possible angles, including, of course, what he knows about the duality of the two realms. When appropriate, he will step boldly into the temporal realm and speak God's truth with authority and discernment—which means he will carefully prioritize the issues he chooses to address and will speak with conviction and force only when God's Word speaks with equal conviction and force. He will consider and assess his audience and context, determining how best to advance the place of God's law in that situation and how best to remind his listeners of the relevance of God's reality and law in their own lives.

The Objectives: Ultimate and Penultimate

In the light of a surrounding evangelical community, for which a conservative-minded Lutheran pastor might well feel some affinity, especially on issues of social policy and morality, it is important to apply the two realms paradigm presented at the outset of this chapter and specify the church's goal or objective for the temporal realm. For the most part, evangelicals have little perplexity about their hopes for the temporal realm. Embracing Niebuhr's fifth and final model for Christian engagement with the culture in which the church works to transform the culture to be in harmony with itself, evangelicals busily champion—though with a bit less optimism than exhibited a few short decades ago—the ideal of a "Christian America." For them, God's purpose is patently obvious: God's reign should extend over the entire earth encompassing every nation and government. The transformation of the culture into a Christian world is the goal for

---

19. It should be obvious that while most pastors encounter opportunities to step into the temporal realm and offer some form of support or service to that realm only on occasion, others in the Office of the Ministry face such realities daily. Chaplains, especially those in a military context, are keenly aware of the challenges posed as they work to balance and honor their responsibilities in both realms. For these men, the sort of clarity and direction offered by a thorough grasp of the two realms and the truths at work in the degree of revelation principle are essential to a successful and manageable ministry. It is quite true that faithful Lutheran chaplains to the armed forces exemplify and embody the dynamic I have outlined here.

many believers, and a Christian America in which government and social policy are all forthrightly and fully based on scripture and Christian principles is the first objective to be achieved. In a sense, of course, the right-thinking and fully formed Lutheran can agree. The ultimate goal of God's activity in this world is certainly the absolute and exhaustive reign of Christ over every corner, creature, and king anywhere in creation. But timing is of the essence. While Lutherans readily acknowledge the ultimate goal of a Christian America, Russia, Brazil, and Nigeria, we also confess that this goal will be attained only at the glorious appearing of Christ on the Last Day. Until then, we wait, we hope, and we live in the tension. And until then, we strive for the penultimate goal of the temporal realm: not a Christian America, but merely a just America that upholds God's law for his creation. This side of the eschatological fulfillment, a just America would be cause enough for rejoicing among God's people.

Keeping the penultimate goal in clear view provides a useful and precise perspective for thinking rightly about issues of church and state interface. The pastor who understands God's purpose for this world and its government does not need to fight for the preservation of Christian privilege within the culture, nor does he become enamored with the Christian credentials of potential candidates or current civil servants. Rather, his driving concern is that the country and its leaders would more nearly conform to God's will for his creation, that is, the law. He is rightly wary of campaigns premised on the "restoration" of America's "godly heritage," does not fawn over political power brokers, and does not swoon like a schoolgirl when courted by candidates seeking to secure a Christian block of votes. Rather, he is content to speak God's word of truth to those who will listen, and earnestly leads his church to engage the world with God's standard of right. With such an attitude, and in light of the discussion about formal engagement with the temporal realm in the previous section, a faithful pastor is sensitive to the possibility that individuals and institutions in the temporal realm may at times seek to co-opt the church, its people, and pastors for its own purposes. Of course, as the church's influence in the wider culture wanes, so will this threat. The temporal realm will see no need to court the church when the church is perceived as inconsequential and irrelevant, or even obstructionist and deleterious. Still, for now, the possibility of the church being pressed into the service of the state persists, and those responsible for leadership in the church must be wary of the church becoming a mere puppet in the machinations and maneuverings of those who wield power in the temporal realm.

Presumably, the temporal realm has some interest in the church's intangible assets: an aura or sense of metaphysical transcendence, spiritual authority, or moral approval that continues to resonate with a significant segment of the population. The state or party that can cloak itself in such spiritual trappings gains no small victory. Or, it may be the more immediate and tangible benefit of garnering the votes of those who still treasure an explicit spiritual or even churchly component within the temporal realm—despite constitutional ambiguity over the extent and content of that churchly component—that interests the left-hand powers. Keeping the penultimate goal in mind, recalling the church's obligation to speak God's truth to the temporal realm, will surely go far in stemming the possibility of the church being made a plaything or patsy of the temporal realm.[20] When the church remembers that the final goal is not the restoration or salvation of America, but the re-creation of the entire created realm, it will be better equipped to withstand temptations to become the pliable stalwart of the state or the crusader bent on saving the nation. Instead, the church can adopt a more reasonable and doctrinally defensible posture toward God's left-hand realm, realizing and teaching that the church's goal for the temporal realm is not to save America, but to preserve the church as faithful to the entire will of God and to promote strong and healthy families

---

20. Of course, others have also issued warnings for the church to guard against being co-opted by the temporal realm. Two representatives of such cautions are William Schumacher, "Civic Participation by Churches and Pastors: An Essay on Two Kinds of Righteousness," *Concordia Journal* 30, no. 3 (July 2004): 175, and Joel Okamoto, "Christians and the Disestablishments of Religion in the United States," in *Witness & Worship in Pluralistic America*, ed. John F. Johnson (St. Louis, MO: Concordia Seminary, 2003), 13.

where Christians are formed into the Christian life. Not only is this the best way for the church to serve the world, but it is also a goal that is far more easily managed than the impossible hope of transforming the state into the church itself. Frankly, the church has more than enough fully to occupy its attention merely striving to maintain the church's faithful confession and practice and to cultivate and habituate its members into this unique way of life. In the gathering storm of individualism, pluralism, and nihilism that is Western culture, these obligations are hardly trivial tasks or realities to be taken for granted. The church needs to worry less about the state of America and pay more attention to the state of the church and her families. The church is tasked to preserve not the nation, but God's truth and God's people.

Conclusion

The topics I used in this chapter to illustrate the application of the two realms paradigm in the life of the church and her pastor are hardly exhaustive. This was never the intent. And I suspect that most readers could readily suggest other more pressing and interesting examples of the interface in action. That is as it should be. The examples considered here grew out of my own experience in the parish and in the classroom, and I have made no attempt to consider every possible situation or even to offer representative scenarios for certain specific types of questions. By nature of the situation and the paradigm itself, an exhaustive list is neither possible nor desirable; not even a suggestion of general areas of interface is appropriate. The objective of the paradigm is to provide a clear and complete principle for thinking and acting in every situation—a principle based not on theory or the thinking of a man or men, but a principle based on God's truth as revealed in his Word. Obviously, situations change with time and place. Thus, nothing is to be gained—in fact, much would be lost—by trying to establish a guidebook or reference list of all possible circumstances in which the spiritual realm intersects deliberately with the temporal realm, followed by the sanctioned and prescribed action to be taken in each situation. Such an approach would not allow for the necessary flexibility that must accompany the paradigm in action. I hope, though, that the situations considered here do present a thoughtful if not provocative sample of how the teaching on two realms operates in actual situations. The beauty and power of the distinction between the temporal and the spiritual realms of God's activity becomes increasingly evident as it is able to be applied fruitfully in each and every new circumstance that is encountered.

Within the church, and certainly within the church as synod or denomination, uniformity or homogeneity in thinking and practice seem to be highly prized and even revered. Perhaps the desire for consistent and standardized practice that evokes unity is part of what drives God's people to develop lists and to assert and defend prescribed courses of action that are always and absolutely to be followed. But faithful theology practiced well is often quite resistant to neat rules or universal guidelines, and the unity that is rightly desired should be sought not in such lists or the creation and preservation of what amounts to canon law. Rather, the church's unity is grounded in her Lord, in her confession, and in the faithful practice that is bound to that confession. But such faithful practice may well be a wildly variegated thing and the unity that binds God's people together should be recognized in the consistent, careful, and thoughtful application of the common binding principle not in conformity to a predetermined set of outcomes. This is the best way to consider and employ the paradigm of the two realms. The paradigm provides a precise framework in which to place questions, clear direction on ways to consider those questions, and points in the direction of answers and actions that are in harmony with the teaching.

Within the church, we recognize that contexts, experiences, influences, and inclinations may well lead different congregations and different pastors to actions that are not outwardly uniform and actually appear wholly incompatible. This need not spell disunity or a failure rightly to confess and act. Behind the equally faithful, but quite divergent actions, there is a common principle and paradigm that is normative, and each faithful outworking of that principle will be recognized as consistent with the teaching, and appropriate in the context. Naturally, such an approach is altogether dependent upon open dialogue among the various congregations and pastors of the church, coupled with a determination to "put the best construction on everything" in the midst of the dynamic interchange as iron sharpens iron and questions and challenges are rightly raised and answered. True unity is present and celebrated when members of Christ's church stand together on Christ's truth, then individually, particularly, and sometimes idiosyncratically apply that truth in their places of service, and finally, encourage one another in the midst of the inevitable multiplicity of resultant applications.

The teaching of the distinction between the two realms is a remarkably versatile tool with significant applications for the life of the church and her called servant, the pastor. While only a representative handful of those applications have been briefly explored here, the importance and usefulness of the paradigm, hopefully by now, should be apparent. It remains for congregations and pastors to embrace and continue the task of rightly applying the principle as they think about their various encounters and interactions with the temporal realm. Of course, the range of implications stemming from the teaching of the two realms is far from complete once one applies it to the church and pastor. Also, for the individual Christian, the distinction and interaction of the two realms is a critical framework and guide for rightly understanding and negotiating the realities of everyday life from the perspective of God's design and intention. Offering evidence of this usefulness, and considering some of the more noteworthy implications, will be the task of the next chapter.

5

Applying the Teaching to the Individual Christian Believer

Good doctrine is a great gift. Far more than a standard of assessment for seminary education, a badge of orthodoxy, or a basis for denominational boasting and squabbling, good doctrine yields tremendous rewards both for the conduct of parish ministry as well as the task of living an ordinary Christian life. Admittedly, this is hardly a universally recognized truth—even many Christians and some clergy would no doubt be skeptical about the claim that the study of doctrine yields fruit for the routine reality of everyday life. Recognized or not, however, the truth remains: good doctrine is invaluable for living a good life. While I am committed to the position that this axiom holds true for every doctrine, I can also acknowledge that the truth may be harder to demonstrate and harder to see for some doctrines than for others. But given the current discussion of the interface between the two realms, the task of advancing my argument of the relevance and pragmatism of doctrine for ordinary life is relatively easy. I do not have to make a case for the applicability and consequence of the *genus majestaticum* for daily living, I have the much easier project of showing the everyday importance of the distinction between the two realms.[1]

The goal of this chapter is to continue what was begun in the previous chapter, but with a particular emphasis on the impact of the teaching not on the church as a whole or on her pastors, but on individual Christians in their ordinary lives. While a chapter division implies a marked divide between the two categories, one must take care not to overdraw the distinction. The church is, of course, the gathering of God's people, so the line between church and individual Christians is arbitrary at best. There is little to be gained by speaking, as so often happens, of the difference between what Christians do "as church" and what they do as individuals. There are no Christian individuals. Every believer, the moment he is brought to faith, is simultaneously brought into relationship with the church and made a member—that is a constituent part—of it. In a very real sense then, when a Christian acts alone in some task—whether honorable or shameful—he acts as an integral part of the church. In his action, the church acts. Whether or not it is intended or acknowledged, every time an individual Christian acts, the church acts. Christians are the church, and the church is Christians. The church and the believer are bound to one another, accountable to one another, and alternately, celebrate or endure one another. So, while it may be convenient or reasonable to group together questions that seem more corporate in nature and to create a separate category that would account for issues or situations that appear to be more individualistic, the distinction is ultimately only theoretical and artificial. Mindful of this caveat, there are several important and interesting applications of the teaching of the two realms as they touch on the individual believer.

In their landmark book, *Resident Aliens*, Stanley Hauerwas and

---

1. For the sake of making my point, though, a case *can* be made even for the former: recognizing that in the hypostatic union, the divine nature imparts godly prerogatives also to the human nature, without abolishing that nature not only confirms and enhances the wonder of receiving Christ's true body and blood at the rail, but affirms the goodness of human flesh, the nearness of Christ to my humanity, the potential of flesh and bones for so much more than anyone can imagine, the great loss to human being incurred at the fall, and may offer concrete motivation and renewed resolve for a believer to honor and care for the body given her by God—thus making a workout at the gym perhaps a bit less onerous!

William Willimon had much to say about the way that Christians should live their lives and the way that churches should function to shape those Christian lives in paths faithful to the church's Lord and proclamation. Of course, the understanding of the Christian life argued by Hauerwas and Willimon is, at critical points, in marked opposition to the teaching of the two realms advocated by Luther—for one thing, the authors assume a comprehensive and unyielding stance of Christian nonviolence that would disallow any possibility of Luther's Christian soldiers. Nevertheless, the authors do have much of value to contribute to the conversation about a Christian's responsibility and obligations when it comes to the surrounding world and its governing institutions. Simply and forcefully, they assert: "The political task of Christians is to be the church rather than to transform the world."[2] The reminder is critically important. Too often, Christians become swept up in political movements allied with virtually every imaginable location along the ideological spectrum. And these same believers will manage to sanctify their political ardor with some, often misinterpreted and misapplied, verses cherry-picked from scripture. Regardless of the legitimacy and morality—or otherwise—of their political objectives, the problem lies in the damage done to their Christian calling. Invariably, Christian confession collapses into political commitments and is overwhelmed so that the clarity of the unique Christian proclamation, and the content of the gospel itself, is compromised and squandered.

As argued in the previous chapter, Christians, on the one hand, must maintain a watchful vigilance against unwittingly being co-opted by the state or the state's agenda, just as on the other hand, they must guard against willfully surrendering themselves and their gospel treasure to the glitter, gold, and goals of the temporal realm and its rulers. Hauerwas and Willimon are right to stress the essential obligation of the Christian first to the church herself. And yet, as *Resident Aliens* understands and argues, when Christians are being the

---

2. Stanley Hauerwas and William Willimon, *Resident Aliens: Life in the Christian Colony* (Nashville, TN: Abingdon, 1989), 38.

church as they should be, this will lead them not to neglect or shun the world, but to enter it in committed service. By now, it should be clear that an essential part of a believer's service to the world will be the performance of obligations toward the state as well as the rest of creation. The Christian's specifically political obligations will be discussed as this chapter proceeds, but a good place to begin is with the wider, more expansive, responsibility of the Christian to the whole of creation that springs from a right understanding of the two realms.

Luther's Other Breakthrough

Though the details are less than certain and remain the subject of much discussion among Luther scholars, every student of the great reformer knows that his theology hinged on his self-described "tower experience." Languishing in the uncertainty and terror provoked by a life of attempted works righteousness, Luther, in the writing of St. Paul, "discovered" the gospel: the righteousness of God is not an achievement to be earned, but a gift to be received. So began the Reformation—at least by most popular accounts. Critical as Luther's gospel breakthrough was for the Reformation and for the entire church and her teaching—and it was vitally critical—that breakthrough was not Luther's only axial moment of enlightenment during those crucial early years of the Reformation. Luther's arrival at the wonder of the gospel fully answered the problem of his life *coram Deo* or in heaven before God, but it was his grasp of the doctrine of vocation that brought him into a meaningful and productive life *coram mundo* or in this world before his fellow creatures. This second great insight made a profound impact on Luther's world, and that impact is felt still today. So significant was Luther's discovery of the doctrine of vocation that it might well be considered his second breakthrough. As with Luther's first great breakthrough to the gospel, the second breakthrough was tied to intense personal struggles and a fascinating narrative. Luther provides some of the details in a letter to his father, Hans.

It was a sudden terrifying thunderstorm that drove Luther into the monastery, of course. Still, a seemingly rash vow to St. Anna may well have been simply the natural next step for the spiritually sensitive and burdened young Luther. In his world, the best chance of finding peace with God came only by embarking on the path of perfection—the route of the saints who renounced worldly affections, treasures, relationships, and obligations and focused entirely on the only relationship that mattered: the one with God. Luther yearned for peace with God, a hope that was all but impossible as a law student. Entrance into a monastery was his best hope. The thunderstorm and his dramatic vow provided the perfect justification to pursue his heart's desire. Hans was less than pleased, effectively losing to the Augustinian Order in Erfurt both his son and his hope for a future retirement. But Martin was in pursuit of God, and no man, not even a father, could interfere, and on this score, the church was firmly on the side of the younger Luther and his vow. Martin focused his intellect and energy on the task at hand. Rising quickly through the ranks, he was trained and ordained. On May 2, 1507, Luther celebrated his first mass. His father had come to terms with Martin's career choice to the extent that he was present for the great event.[3] In his letter to Hans, Luther recounts the heart of what happened after the mass was complete:

> For I remember very well that after we were reconciled and you were [again] talking with me, I told you that I had been called by terrors from heaven and that I did not become a monk of my own free will and desire, still less to gain gratification of the flesh, but that I was walled in by the terror and the agony of sudden death and forced by necessity to take the vow. Then you said, "Let us hope that it was not an illusion and a deception." That word penetrated to the depths of my soul and stayed there, as if God had spoken by your lips, though I hardened my heart against you and your word as much as I could. You said something else too. When in filial confidence I upbraided you for your wrath, you suddenly retorted with a reply so fitting and so much to the point that I have hardly ever in all my life heard any man say anything which struck me so forcibly and stayed with me so long. "Have you not also heard," you said, "that parents are to be obeyed?" But I was so sure of my own righteousness that in you I heard only a man, and boldly ignored you; though in my heart I could not ignore your word.[4]

3. Scott H. Hendrix, *Martin Luther: Visionary Reformer* (New Haven, CT and London: Yale University Press, 2015), 38.
4. *LW* 48, 332.

Martin refused, or simply was unable, to acknowledge it at the time, but his father did know best. Hans had given full expression to what his son eventually would learn was the heart of God's truth.

The second breakthrough is the importance, and more than that, the beauty of fulfilling the work that God gives each person by virtue of that specific person's relationships and responsibilities in life. It would come to be called the doctrine of vocation. For Luther, the foundation for understanding and fulfilling a vocation must be the realities of birth, marriage, work, and community. In other words, the places and roles in which a person lives are the setting, the definition and direction, and the meaning of one's purpose in life—one's vocations. The person who does such things, does God's will, and thus, honors his Creator and serves well his fellow creation. Thus, Luther would learn rightly to evaluate his sacred oath to St. Anna:

> For my vow was not worth a fig, since by taking it I withdrew myself from the authority and guidance of the parent [to whom I was subject] by God's commandment; indeed, it was a wicked vow, and proved that it was not of God not only because it was a sin against your authority, but because it was not absolutely free and voluntary.[5]

If one thinks only in terms of Luther's first breakthrough, it would be easy to conclude that the reformer's quarrel with monasticism centered in the inevitable works righteousness and self-justification bred in the orders. It is clear from his own testimony, however, that Luther's repudiation of the monastic system was equally, if not more, driven by his realization that monasticism gutted the doctrine of vocation. Luther treasured his standing before God by grace in the gospel of Christ, but he also learned to treasure the joy of living in his God-given vocations in the created world. Monasticism destroyed both:

> So Paul also predicted when he said that men would become disobedient to parents. This fits the monks and priests exactly, especially those who under the pretense of piety and the guise of serving God withdraw themselves from the authority of their parents, as though there were any

---

5. Ibid.

other service of God except the keeping of his commandments, which includes obedience to parents.[6]

Living as an obedient son was, of course, but one of Luther's vocations, but it served well to illustrate the sharp and fundamental contrast between living within a cloister, or living within a vocation.

If the doctrine of vocation, the affirmation and pursuit of the tasks given to each person in the context of that person's family, work, and community relationships and responsibilities truly qualifies for "breakthrough" status, one would expect to see Luther address the ideas often. He does.[7] But, for the sake of brevity, I shall limit myself to one other illustrative sample, this one with confessional status:

> Let all of them come forward with their many, great, laborious, and difficult works and boast. Let us see whether they can produce a single work that is greater and nobler than obeying father and mother, which God has ordained and commanded next to obedience to his own majesty. If God's Word and will are placed first and are observed, nothing ought to be considered more important than the will and word of our parents. . . .
>
> If this could be impressed on the poor people, a servant girl would dance for joy and praise and thank God; and with her careful work, for which she receives sustenance and wages, she would obtain a treasure such as those who are regarded as the greatest saints do not have. Is it not a tremendous honor to know this and to say, "If you do your daily household chores, that is better than the holiness and austere life of all the monks?" Moreover, you have the promise that whatever you do will prosper and fare well. How could you be more blessed or lead a holier life, as far as works are concerned? In God's sight it is actually faith that makes a person holy; it alone serves God, while our works serve people.[8]

The precise location of faith *coram Deo* and works *coram mundo* provides a succinct and lucid summation of the dynamic reality that lies at the center of the Christian life—and that plays out in the two realms. Righteous by grace through faith in Christ, the believer is delivered

---

6. Ibid., 335–36.
7. After years of neglect, in the last decades, Luther's doctrine of vocation has received increasing attention. Gustaf Wingren deserves credit for standing at the front of this reclamation of vocation. One can gain much by consulting his classic: Gustaf Wingren, *Luther on Vocation*, trans. Carl C. Rasmussen (Eugene, OR: Wipf and Stock, 1957).
8. KW, 402, 406. LC Ten Commandments, 116, 145–48.

back to the created world to serve fellow creatures by fulfilling her vocations in a life of good works. Good works are deeds and gestures redeemed by Christ and done in harmony with God's will for his creation. Luther made clear that the monastic life failed on both counts.

Creation as the Object

Created not to flee the world, but to serve it as a responsible and careful ruler of the creation, one lives according to God's purpose when one engages with this world, undertaking and fulfilling the tasks of various vocations with purpose. Seen from the perspective of the two realms, a Christian who works to accomplish her vocations is simply striving to meet her creaturely responsibilities within God's good temporal realm. The work she does is certainly God-pleasing, and significant in its own right by virtue of the fact that it serves the temporal realm. Thinking in terms of Luther's three estates or Bonhoeffer's supportive expansion into the four mandates leads to a greater appreciation of the scope and importance of each person's varying vocations. Whether at home, at work, in the government, or in the church, the believer strives to use the gifts and talents given for the good of those around. This work is good and holy and godly for its own sake. Mundane and secular as these tasks may be, they need no spiritualizing or "Christianizing" to be made good or worthy of Christian pursuit. Work done in the world for the world does not need transformation or augmentation to be worthy of Christian attention. Work done for the good of the neighbor and in the name of upholding and enhancing the wonder of the creation does not need to be redirected or reconfigured to bring praise to God the Creator. Work done for the sake of the creation is its own end. To seek to spiritualize the work of vocation merely diminishes and trivializes both the work and the creation—an affront to the God who created, loved, and celebrated his remarkable handiwork.

There is a tendency among Christians to cast their lives of service in terms of their relationship with God—all the more when that work is done in concert with other believers and explicitly in the name of the church. Thus, the congregational youth group embarks on a week-long adventure rehabbing a house in an impoverished neighborhood and does so for the sake of Jesus and in the name of his church as their neon t-shirts loudly proclaim. They serve the neighbor because they love Jesus, and they are not timid about making known the motivations for their sacrificial labor—even to the neighbor. And the "senior saints" group works under the blaze of an August sun, distributing water bottles to parched fair-goers, with the bottles themselves offering a pointed declaration of the reason behind the beneficent and welcome gift: "This free water comes from the One who wants to give you the free gift of living water." The natural disaster strikes and in the aftermath, congregation members don their Christian-service-t-shirt uniforms and stream into the neighborhood to serve Jesus and look for ways to "share the gospel." This is clearly an advance from the problem of monastic detachment and retreat from the world. In every scenario, the believer is exactly where she should be: in the world, working for the world. Yet, a lingering problem remains, one stubborn vestige of monastic thinking. While done in the world, the work is still aimed—at least in thought and motive—toward God. The work in the world is given a spiritual veneer or meaning to enhance or Christianize it. Such thinking entirely misses the point of the two realms. With exceptional clarity, Gustaf Wingren identified this problem in an essay from 1956:

> In heaven Christ reigns with His Gospel, that is to say, with pure giving and grace. Man enters this heavenly Kingdom through faith, which receives and lays hold on the Gospel and thereby on Christ Himself. But the neighbor lives on earth, and one does not believe and trust in him. One does not receive salvation from him, but rather serves the neighbor in one's daily work. We may set forth the following proposition: If man seeks to take the *works* which God commands him to do and bring these works *before God*, man thereby abolishes God's order both in "heaven" and on "earth". For in heaven the Gospel reigns alone. Here to seek to place works *before God* as a means of justification is an attempt to depose Christ from His throne. Man allows his works to compete with the King of heaven. But at the same time *the neighbor* is pushed aside in the *earthly* kingdom, for works are not done for the neighbor's sake, but in order that I might

adorn myself with them before God. Christ is "dethroned" in heaven and the neighbor is "dethroned" on earth.[9]

The good works done within Christian vocations are done not for God's benefit, but for the benefit of the neighbor. The fact that a neighbor is in need is reason enough for a Christian to intervene and offer service. Such work certainly honors the Creator whose creation is being served, but that loving action does not need a Christian foundation or justification for it to be good, right, and worthy of Christian participation.

In an otherwise insightful and helpful book covering the doctrines of church and ministry, Kurt Marquart ventures some advice for the church's social efforts which serves as a further illustration of the failure fully to adopt and appreciate a robust understanding of the temporal realm:

> Needless to say, our modern world with its massive miseries offers ample opportunity for the exercise of love's healing. The relief of human wretchedness today calls for an inventive resourcefulness. But congregations, acting singly or together with others, need to take care that their diaconic labors truly proceed from the altar and lead to the altar, so that they are not perceived either within or without simply as ecclesiastical extensions of the welfare bureaucracy.[10]

While it is certainly true that God's good gospel gifts given at the altar prompt much charitable work and may well prove to be a tool in the neighbor's reception of saving grace and faith at the altar, the works done in the world remain in the world and accomplish their own ends there in the world. A fear of the church resembling other mere arms of welfare bureaucracy reflects a poor understanding of the work done in the world. Such efforts are entirely sufficient when done in accord with God's justice and for the good of the neighbor. One does not need to introduce or highlight a peculiarly Christian imprint for a work to be worthy of Christians either as the corporate church or as

9. Gustaf Wingren, "Justification by Faith in Protestant Thought," *Scottish Journal of Theology* 9 (Dec 1956): 375–76.
10. Kurt Marquart, *The Church and Her Fellowship, Ministry, and Governance* (Fort Wayne, IN: The International Foundation for Lutheran Confessional Research, 1990), 140.

individual believers. The work does not need to be "sanctified" with Jesus-branding and Jesus-packaging. The Christian altar—sacred and essential as it is—does not make a work for the neighbor's sake worth doing and it does not define or give meaning to that work. Rather, the need of the neighbor, a fellow creature, is sufficient justification, explanation, and connotation for the works Christians do in the world. The creation itself is the object and the end of Christian vocation and acts of service.

A Christian lives her life for the sake of the world around her. The recognition of this truth is perhaps the single greatest application for and impact on individual believers when the truth about the two realms is rightly comprehended and taught. The clear distinction between life's realities in the spiritual realm *coram Deo* and life's responsibilities in the temporal realm *coram mundo* sets the Christian free to engage wholeheartedly in a virtually limitless array of worthy and necessary work for the sake of the world's exceedingly great sorrows and suffering as well as mundane tasks that simply need to be done for the good of another creature. This work is not, in any sense, a form of social gospel—in truth, it is not the gospel at all! This work is not the proclamation of forgiveness of sins in Christ, and does not pretend to be. Such work is an expression of love certainly, which always finds its origin and fulfillment in God's love in Christ toward his creation, but it is not the gospel. The work is simply a believer's effort to do what she was put on this earth to do. Knowing the gospel, the Christian strives to fulfill the purpose for which she was created—she serves her neighbor, she does her vocation. The work she does in and for the surrounding creation is God-pleasing in that it adheres to God's will for his creatures, but it is not salvific, nor even done with an eye turned toward the Creator. With both eyes focused together, the Christian sees what God sees: a world in need, neighbors to be served, tasks to be accomplished, a creation to be celebrated. For the sake of the creation, the Christian steps into the joy and the misery—and serves.

Living a Confessional Life

All that has been so far argued in this chapter is smartly and comprehensively articulated in the Augsburg Confession and its Apology. Of course, this may well be glaringly self-evident, but it is nonetheless worth observing and corroborating with a quotation or two. Article 16 of the Augustana takes up the problem of the Christian's relation to the secular realm and provides clear direction that serves as a succinct summary of the position I have been trying to establish:

> Concerning public order and secular government it is taught that all political authority, orderly government, laws, and good order in the world are created and instituted by God and that Christians may without sin exercise political authority; be princes and judges; pass sentences and administer justice according to imperial and other existing laws; punish evildoers with the sword; wage just wars; serve as soldiers; buy and sell; take required oaths; possess property; be married; etc. Condemned here are the Anabaptists who teach that none of the things indicated above is Christian.[11]

What should not be missed here is the thoroughgoing endorsement of the temporal realm, and in particular, the institution established by God to administer that realm. When a prince, a peace officer, or even a soldier is doing his work obediently and justly, he is doing a good and god-pleasing vocation. It is holy work. In marked contrast to the errant conclusions of the Anabaptists, the Confession is explicit: Christians are not to reject, shun, or even merely tolerate the temporal realm with a measured ambivalence. Rather, they should launch themselves into the temporal realm with assured abandon. The article continues with a forthright dismissal of the monastic system that coheres exactly with Luther's own position considered above:

> Also condemned are those who teach that Christian perfection means physically leaving house and home, spouse and child, and refraining from the above-mentioned activities. In fact, the only true perfection is true fear of God and true faith in God. For the gospel teaches an internal, eternal reality and righteousness of the heart, not an external, temporal

---

11. Kolb and Wengert, 48, AC XVI, 1–3.

one. The gospel does not overthrow secular government, public order, and marriage but instead intends that a person keep all this as a true order of God and demonstrate in these walks of life Christian love and true good works according to each person's calling.[12]

The fact that "government, public order, and marriage" all combine to comprise "a true order of God" explains and grounds the entire argument. Once one has acknowledged the divine origin and divine approval of the material world, vigorous participation in that world and its orders must be recognized as the way of life that is most truly Christian.

When Melanchthon penned his detailed defense of the Augsburg Confession in the Apology, he ended the section relating to the church by affirming once again that there is no animosity, antagonism, or even dividing wall between God's two realms. Christians, he contends, even Christian pastors, live and fully participate in both realms:

> And it is permissible for Christians to use civil ordinances, just as they use the air, light, food, and drink. For as this universe and the fixed movements of the stars are truly orders of God and are preserved by God, so legitimate governments are truly orders of God and are preserved and defended by God against the devil.[13]

Particularly interesting is the way that the author of the Augustana and the Apology invokes the farthest reaches of the created material realm, the stars themselves, in asserting the divine origin and ordering of temporal authority, the institution particularly tasked to practice the dominion requisite in the commission first expressed to Adam. The created world is God's world, and those who care for it and administer it are doing work fully consistent with God's will; in fact, they are appointed for their work and upheld in their work by God himself. The temporal realm matters to God and to the Christian; and the Christian who lives within God's design and purpose will give herself fully to the work of serving and enhancing the creation through her vocations, whatever they may be. So, it is that when the Christian endeavors

---

12. Kolb and Wengert, 48–50, AC XVI, 4–5.
13. Ibid., 183 Ap VII and VIII, 50.

faithfully to "be the church" in her own living, she will inevitably decide, speak, and act in ways for which she may well be deemed an activist for the sake of the world.

The activism of a Christian will no doubt assume many forms. Between the circumstances of time and place, the peculiar arrangement of genetics and experience for each person, and the latitude inherent in interpreting God's will, every Christian will enter and engage the world in ways that are quite rightly idiosyncratic and unique. There are simply too many variables to offer a standard list of "Christian" causes. Neither is there a prescribed formula for Christian presence in the world. As C. S. Lewis puts it, we must understand that

> Christianity has not, and does not profess to have, a detailed political programme [sic] for applying "Do as you would be done by" to a particular society at a particular moment. It could not have. It is meant for all men at all times and the particular programme which suited one place or time would not suit another. And, anyhow, that is not how Christianity works. When it tells you to feed the hungry it does not give you lessons in cookery.[14]

One should not expect every Christian to agree on the recipe to be followed, or even whether a meal is to be prepared, but every Christian should recognize a hungry neighbor and realize that his Christian confession compels him to help meet the need of that neighbor. Christian activists may not necessarily march in rallies, lobby lawmakers, boycott businesses, or buy billboards, but they will give of themselves for the sake of their fellow creatures around, and most especially, near them.

The Preservation of Creation

There is significant latitude in conceiving and practicing the First Article, that is temporal realm, activism that should mark the life of the follower of Christ. Still, the choice of potential causes in which a Christian might invest, and the course of his action within that area

14. C. S. Lewis, *Mere Christianity* (New York: Macmillan, 1943), 78–79.

of service are not entirely subject to the whims or inclinations of the individual. In truth, they are not actually a matter of individual choice or interpretation at all. While each individual certainly will have varying opportunities, capabilities, and interests, those individualistic factors always are, or should be, harnessed and directed by that person's place within the community of faith. That is to say, God through his church will guide each person in the pursuit of upright and admirable avenues of service. Thus, a specific believer's degree of "passion" for some idea, agenda, cause, or need is frankly not particularly relevant or important. It is entirely possible that a believer might experience no exceptional burning interest or concern for the work she commits to do—beyond the realization that she has a creaturely responsibility purposefully to serve those around, and exhaustively to use her gifts to do so. The church, the community of faith, will assist each Christian to see what must be seen: a lack in the surrounding world, and a path to satisfy that lack. Once the need is recognized, the believer identifies in himself or herself the skills, talents, and resources available to meet that need. So, a young Christian man may not harbor a compelling concern for the homeless in his city, and in unguarded moments, may even admit an inability to see the homeless people he encounters while en route to various venues in the city as anything more than an annoyance and a catalyst for fleeting feelings of guilt. Nevertheless, at the insistence of the church, that young man is persuaded to give of his time and money each month to work in a shelter providing food, warmth, and encouragement to the very men and women he would ordinarily deftly circumnavigate when walking the city's streets. One need not wait for a passion, or even an identifiable interest, to manifest itself before choosing to take action for the sake of fellow creatures. The wisdom of the church, the neighbor's need, and one's own resources are the best criteria for determining the right field of service.

Christians seeking direction and wisdom in selecting suitable outlets for their energies and appropriate beneficiaries of the resources entrusted to them must take into account the counsel and guidance of the church as it is present for them in other believers, but especially in the local congregation. In turn, the guidance that is provided must be normed and shaped by the clear purposes and objectives that define the temporal realm. Once again, vigilance is essential lest service that enjoys an appearance of spirituality or religiosity supplant more mundane and world-bound avenues of care for fellow creatures. The best guide is the simple division between the realms, and the respective concerns and responsibilities of each. It is important to remember that in the temporal realm—in other words, in the day-to-day world of routine life that occupies most of a person's waking hours—it is the law that is normative, the goal or objective is a world that operates according to the law, and creatures should strive for the promotion of justice. These are not concessionary goals or diminished, second-tier purposes and directives for life—even a Christian life. The fact that spiritual aspects are not evident, that one is not working for "the gospel," or that Christ is not explicitly mentioned as foundation or impetus does not disallow or devalue a Christian's pursuit of specifically temporal objectives. Striving for the extension of God's law, fighting for the application of justice, and working toward peace serve as clarion standards for the believer intent on meeting his creaturely obligations. These are, of course, exceedingly temporal, penultimate, goals that might well be pursued by a moral unbeliever with a social conscience. But, this fact is not a slight or disparagement of these goals. These are life targets and purposes altogether fitting for a Christian.

In conversation with other believers in the church, then, the Christian affirms the pursuit of temporal realm realities and begins to determine which of those realities will occupy his own attention. While a multitude of needs will confront the aware and conscientious Christian, not all needs are created equal. An elderly woman across the street with an overgrown backyard needs help pruning and clearing, but the neighbor next door with a fire on his deck has a somewhat more pressing need. Migratory birds need the preservation of nesting habitats in subarctic taiga regions, but the newly arrived family of immigrants who escaped the chaos of civil war with little more than their lives need to establish new lives in a new community. The urgency of the need, the creatures that are threatened, the level of other resources already being directed toward the need, the sufficiency of personal resources available to invest, and the degree of potential impact one can make in alleviating the need are important factors that should be considered when one tries to determine where to begin in serving the staggering, multiplying needs of the temporal realm. There is nothing formulaic or determined about such decisions. One family considers the needs they see, asks the guiding questions, and adopts several children with special needs. Another couple does the same, and sacrifices personal savings earmarked for vacation and home renovation to put a new roof on a Christian school in Haiti. Another Christian sees the needs in the world around and volunteers to teach an ESL course at the community library, and another spends several days every month encouraging and materially supporting young mothers who have opted not to terminate an unplanned pregnancy. Still another provides free legal counsel and representation to immigrants overwhelmed by bewildering bureaucratic and arbitrary legislative regulations that threaten to shatter their families. All of these, and thousands of other, scenarios of selfless service result from Christians grasping and living the impact of the teaching of the two realms.

There is a distinctively Christian component to such temporal realm work. Christian believers and their unbelieving neighbors will, of course, both see needs in the world, and believers will not be alone in sacrificing personal resources in an effort to address the needs that they see. Yet, as Christians intentionally hear and heed God's law in their efforts to alleviate suffering and establish justice, their pursuits will be prioritized and guided by that directing law in distinctively Christian ways. A Christian will recognize that protecting and advocating for an infant is immeasurably more important than serving as protector and advocate for a baby seal. A Christian knows that though both are creatures of God, a human and a seal simply do not share equal standing or value in God's plan. An unbeliever, on the contrary, may well chafe at such a distinction, deeming all higher life forms as essentially equal; in fact, a person who lives without a Christian confession might even suggest that an "endangered" animal species actually has more value than an "unwanted" child. Further, while Christians will rightly take into account the environmental impact of choices they make when purchasing or disposing of products, they will also recognize that it is far better to use several thousand dollars of their personal finances to supply safe drinking water to a village in Africa than to use those same funds to retrofit their home with solar panels in an attempt to reduce carbon emissions. Christians follow God's priorities and rank needs according to God's criteria. They do not in a shallow and mindless manner join the parade of populist causes of the pagan world around them, no matter how noble or sentimental those causes may appear. God's will sets the agenda.

Of course, even when united in their commitment to God's normative will as revealed in his law, Christians will nevertheless hold different opinions regarding the priority of one cause over another. Even among believers who have coalesced in their effort to address a singular, well-defined need, there will yet be widely different ideas and approaches regarding how best to solve the problem. Some Christians combat the evil of abortion by regularly protesting at the location where the destruction is done. Others lobby lawmakers or work on the campaigns of those candidates committed to changing errant law. Others will build, support, or serve in homes for mothers who have determined to give birth to their children in spite of extraordinarily difficult personal circumstances. And others will write, speak, or produce material in an effort to educate, influence, and motivate the thinking and acting of people with regard to the wrong of abortion. According to their skills, resources, perspective, vocational responsibilities, and community of believers, each believer acts in ways congruent with God's will. The example of the widely varied yet appropriate responses to the need presented by abortion is illustrative of the richly varied ways that believers will always respond to whatever particular need they identify in the world. Obviously, there is nothing to be gained by comparing or ranking the various responses. Christian wisdom encourages believers to celebrate each of the manifold manifestations of mercy and compassion toward God's creation that are expressed by God's people—regardless of their own personal inclinations or thoughts.

Into the Voting Booth

Christians will give themselves fully to serve and preserve the creation all around them. This is their purpose, according to the first great commission of Genesis 1:28, their *raison d'être*. God creates and redeems his people for the sake of the entire creation. The individual Christian's right relationship with the whole of the surrounding creation is an essential component of the teaching of the two realms. And while the Christian's temporal realm objective is the preservation of the creation and not the preservation of the nation per se, the relationship of the believer to the nation—particularly to the government of the nation—is a topic that rightly demands, and now receives, further attention. The Christian believer is altogether interested in the temporal realm and committed to its right functioning, thus that same believer must be equally interested in and committed to the institution established to guide and provide for that realm. Government can never provoke a response of indifference, much less animosity or contempt from a Christian. Rather, the believer will always consider and honor the divine origin and continued divine preservation of the government and those in positions of civil authority. This attitude has always been an essential aspect of Christian teaching, presented and evidenced by Jesus, and then, reinforced by both Paul and Peter. Of course, this is also the foundational doctrine that undergirds all that Luther taught under what we call the two realms. God is the source of all authority, thus that authority should be considered accordingly.

The core principles and subsequent teaching about God's twofold way of working in this world through the temporal and spiritual realms with their respective institutions established for the oversight and care of each have never changed. By definition, God's truth about the world and its arrangement does not evolve over time. But the application of that truth to the contemporary situation is also, by definition, always moving and adjusting. Each generation of believers must confess God's truth faithfully by applying that truth to their immediate context and shifting situations. It is true that people are prone to overestimate what they see as the unparalleled singularity of their particular era's brilliance, achievements, decadence, failures, or needs, but it is also true that the world is never quite the same as it was in a previous generation. The world is in a constant state of flux, so the application of God's truth to that world must be comparably mutable. Paul's relationship with his government bore no resemblance to Luther's relationship with his government, and both are out of step with the sort of interactions Christians in the contemporary West have with their governments. We do not live in imperial Rome, nor in the loosely confederated princedoms of Luther's day. Without getting ensnared in parsing and nuancing terms, or over-defining the differences in political systems, most readers find themselves living under some form of Western representative democracy. It is a different world, indeed.

In Paul's world as well as in Luther's, everyone from princes to plebeians knew that authority came from beyond this world. Kings ruled by divine right—however that divinity might be named. For more than fifteen hundred years, Paul's strong declaration would have received hearty affirmation from all but a handful of dissidents: "For there is no authority except from God, and those which exist are established by God."[15] That certain, near-universal conviction would not survive the rise of the Enlightenment. In the wake of Descartes and his heirs, every part of the world changed—including its understanding of government. In a modern, enlightened, democracy, authority does not come from God—it comes from the people. And while Christians living in those democracies may rightly view the *demos* as simply another avenue for the exercise of God's ultimate authority, that final

15. Romans 13:1 (NASB).

divine source of authority is certainly not required, much less recognized by the democracy itself. In the United States, there is no greater authority than "we the people." The people themselves are the final arbiters of law, order, and ultimately, truth itself. The inherent dissonance between a biblical understanding of governmental authority and that of a modern democracy becomes glaringly apparent as the democracy's authority-wielding populace becomes increasingly less theistic in conviction and action. Such is the situation in many Western-style democracies. Meanwhile, too many Christians are gaping and wringing their hands in bewilderment, trying to comprehend what has "gone wrong" with the nation's moral compass. They forget that according to the nation's own constitution, morality has no other source or norm than "we the people." It never has. The world is always changing, and yet, God's truth does not change. Acknowledged or not, Paul and Luther are quite right: all authority is from God, and the government with which one must interact is always God's government.

There is, though, another critical aspect to consider as Christians come to terms with their government. Unlike the situations faced by Paul, Luther, and every intervening saint, Christians who live in a democracy in a very real sense *are* the government. This reality is largely lost on citizens who seem to have no difficulty distinguishing themselves from the government, which is, to them, little more than an inefficient, imperious, often onerous, and always wholly-other institution that unfortunately must be endured. Yet, the truth remains that in a democracy, the electorate is part—the foundational part—of the government. Christians living in the United States and other Western democracies need, first of all, to recognize their distinct vocational responsibilities in the state. Yes, they join Peter and Paul in praying for their leaders, paying taxes, and showing fitting honor to their leaders, but they must do more. The Augsburg Confession could summarize a Christian's obligations toward the state in a single sentence, qualified by the narrowest exception: "Christians, therefore, are obliged to be subject to political authority and to obey its commands and laws in all that may be done without sin. But if a command of the political authority cannot be followed without sin, one must obey God rather than any human beings (Acts 5[:29])."[16] That was the extent of a Christian's responsibility. Today, much more is expected of Christians living in democracies. Today, they must also vote. And when the voting is done, they must continue the active pursuit of their vocational obligations by staying abreast of governmental actions and decisions and routinely doing what they can to influence and even shape those decisions and actions. Voting is not an option or a mere privilege that a Christian may choose to exercise—it is a holy obligation. Voting with wisdom about candidates and issues is a further aspect of that obligation. Not only can a Christian sin against the Creator's will by failing to vote, she can also violate that will by how she votes. There is nothing theologically or morally neutral about a voting booth.

Once it is proposed that a Christian has a responsibility to vote and to vote according to a standard other than individual intuition, it is not long before the obfuscating objections are raised. With so many pressing social, environmental, economic, and security needs and concerns confronting the informed Christian voter, how can anyone suggest that any one issue is more compelling than another? If a case is made that Christians should vote with the aim of ending abortion on demand, then the need to address urban blight, chronic poverty, and racial injustice will be offered as equally legitimate and countervailing problems. Then, concerns about securing national borders, the erosion of religious freedom, and the redefinition of morality will be asserted as additional issues that should warrant a Christian's attention and direct a believer's voting choices. Add concerns about environmental protection, immigration law inequities and injustices, and militaristic foreign policies and the list becomes overwhelming. With so many needs and so many opinions about those needs and the relative importance of each compared to the rest, it seems reasonable and right that relativity must win and no peculiarly

16. KW, 50, AC XVI, 6–7.

Christian approach to voting can exist. But obscurity and a levelling of all moral questions is not the end of the discussion.

Just as there is guidance for a Christian as she responds to the needs she encounters in her world, so there is guidance for the way in which she fulfills her obligation to vote. Unlike the rest of life, in the voting booth, the individual skills, opportunities, and resources available to the voter are essentially irrelevant. What must guide the Christian's vote is her desire and responsibility to encourage and influence the temporal realm to do well what it is supposed to do. In that light, the Christian considers each ballot issue and each candidate, striving to determine the degree to which the passage of a given ballot measure or the election of a particular candidate is likely to honor and advance the normative will of God. The extension and application of God's law into the world is the one and only driving concern when a Christian exercises the franchise. The potential for self-interested gain, whether personal economic benefits, or other perceived advantages or disadvantages for oneself or one's group must not be considered as pertinent factors. A believer's vote, like every vocation the Christian undertakes, is done for the sake of the surrounding creation, and not for self. When sorting out candidates and issues, direction comes from the standards and priorities presented and implicit in God's revealed will. The preservation of wildlife habitats, fair labor laws, just immigration practices, and the curbing of violence and the preservation of life all matter, but they do not matter in the same way or with the same urgency. God's will, made clear in his law and taught in scripture, is unwavering: the protection of human life matters more than securing human comfort; the pursuit of justice matters more than the pursuit of a desirable standard of living; compassion shown to the marginalized or weak matters more than national self-interest and prosperity. These are simple standards that should be evident to anyone attending to the teaching of Christ and his church.

It should also be evident that when God's law is directing the Christian's voting and further political activity, then it is all but impossible that any single political party or social action group will align perfectly or even substantially with a Christian's own objectives and standards. A Christian must shape his political outlook and gain his personal political platform not from politicians, pundits, personalities, PACs, or even personal preferences, but exclusively from Christ and his church. Yes, public policy gets complicated, and two Christians both fully committed to God's will and justice can rightly engage in lively and multifaceted debates about how best to bring those sacred objectives more fully into the world's reality. There is no single Christian position on appropriate minimum wage laws, farm subsidies, or auto emission standards. Nevertheless, for a Christian intent on the pursuit of God's standard of justice, there are certain social and political issues that loom large with a relative weight and importance that justifiably eclipse all others. Yes, there are Christians who will decry the thought that they should ever be compelled into being a "single-issue voter," and some believers will renounce what they see as the narrow and confining strictures of a litmus test issue that seeks to define Christian political behavior. I sympathize with this concern. The world in which we live is richly layered, endlessly intriguing, and rarely reduced to one dimension. Still, even granting the complexity of the political landscape and conceding the need for Christian awareness and action on behalf of a host of legitimate issues, a believer needs to recognize that her cultural situation may drastically curtail her available options and curb the social/political latitude she might otherwise enjoy. Complaints about single-issue voting or a litmus test issue fade into trivial inconsequence in the face of a culture that has convinced itself that killing a child is a moral choice.

The privilege and responsibility of ordinary citizens able to participate in government through their vote is a phenomenon that would have been inconceivable to Luther, it is true. Yet, as the forgoing discussion marked with cultural awareness, measured nuance, and immediate relevance demonstrates, Luther's teaching on the two realms is in no way obsolete. The truth of Luther's powerful paradigm is confirmed by its ability meaningfully and incisively to shape the thinking and action of Christians living in modern democratic nations.

In such contexts, the duality of the two realms does not need to be discarded or even recalibrated; rather, it needs to be endorsed and practiced.

The Denial of Rights

Named by an ultimate citizenship in God's kingdom, and defined by an eschatological hope that surpasses and supplants the aspirations and promises of every human-derived community and cause, Christians inevitably find themselves at odds with other voters. They do not see the world the way that others see it. Believers hold an allegiance vastly more demanding and compelling than patriotic loyalty to any tribe or nation, adhering to standards and striving for objectives that not only frequently challenge, but often flatly repudiate those of their countrymen. One important example of the irreconcilable disparity that exists between Christian and non-Christian ways of seeing the world is the contradictory way that each group understands the concept of basic human rights. In the West, since the days of Descartes, the individual has reigned as the center of reality. With the enthronement of the sacred and sovereign individual has come the enshrinement of the notion of inalienable rights. In the modern world, there are few ideas as universally assumed and revered as that of foundational, essential human rights. People may argue about which rights belong on the "essential" list, but of the existence of such a list, there is no doubt whatsoever.[17] But Christians do doubt—or at least they should. Of course, it is certainly true that not all Christians actually recognize the disjunction that should characterize the difference between their own assessment of individual rights over and against that of unbelievers. Dulled by decades of comfortable Constantinianism and content to join their fellow countrymen in cultivating their rights to life, liberty, and at least the pursuit of ever-

---

17. The suggestion that access to affordable health care be considered a basic human right may find general support, but what about a right to receive prompt service at a fast-food drive-through, or a right to express one's chosen sexual identity in whatever way an individual may prefer? A society that inculcates an attitude of entitlement generates a citizenry ready to make remarkable claims in the name of an ever-expanding list of basic rights.

elusive happiness, it has probably never occurred to most Western Christians that the very notion of human rights is in any way problematic for a follower of Christ. Notwithstanding such widespread ignorance, the truth is that a commitment to basic human rights is not a Christian idea or teaching.[18] Christians have no rights, and they would have it no other way.

All that a Christian has, every possession, every honor, every experience, every talent, every skill, every friend, her family, her body, even her life itself all comes to her as gift and nothing more. She lives always and only as the recipient of the Creator's merciful and generous giving, unable to assert a claim to anything and powerless to demand anything. The Christian knows that she does not have a right to hold property, to enjoy freedom, to pursue happiness, or even to live. She only has what God grants by grace. God is beholden to no man, no law, and no principle. From the standpoint of Christian faith then, there are no rights—only dispensations and privileges granted. These dispensations extend also to the privileges granted to the individual citizens of a particular nation, under the guise of human rights. Thus, the first ten amendments to the United States Constitution are for the believer not a Bill of Rights, but a wonderful array of privileges granted by God through the state. The import of this argument is significant, and not merely a matter of academic or theological posturing in the name of rank sensationalism or gratuitous provocation of the reader. A Christian who has learned to see his life and his world through the lens of grace received rather than rights deserved will approach all that he does in fresh, often unexpected, and even disarmingly powerful ways. He will live like a follower of Christ in the world!

The goal of jettisoning talk of rights among Christians is to lead and equip those Christians to enter into their Lord's temporal realm not for the sake of themselves but for the sake of those around them. So, while the believer does not assert her right to life or liberty or even think in terms of her own rights, she will work tirelessly to assure the gifts of

---

18. Fuller development and discussion of this claim can be found in my essay, "Individualism as the Insistence on My Rights," in *The American Mind Meets the Mind of Christ*, Robert Kolb, ed. (St. Louis, MO: Concordia, 2010), 44–53.

life and liberty to those who are being denied these gracious privileges. And while the Christian will use every available tool, including lobbying legislators, invoking legal protections, and asserting "rights" granted by the state in the pursuit of justice and compassion for a poor, powerless, discarded, ignored, or silent fellow creature, she will not use those same means for the sake of herself or even her church. Luther made the same argument in his essay "Temporal Authority: To What Extent It Should Be Obeyed" published in 1523. "A Christian," wrote Luther, "should be so disposed that he will suffer every evil and injustice without avenging himself; neither will he seek legal redress in the courts but have utterly no need of temporal authority and law for his own sake."[19] However, when it is the neighbor's life and livelihood that is at risk, then Luther offers different counsel altogether: "On behalf of others, however, he may and should seek vengeance, justice, protection, and help, and do as much as he can to achieve it."[20] Naturally, a certain reciprocity comes into play here. And while the Christian's defense of others and vice versa can be quite appropriate, care must be exercised lest the church's uniquely selfless and others-centered confession in the world be compromised or trivialized. Luther argues that when acting appropriately, the government itself should also come to the aid of the maltreated believer, but should it fail, the believer has no recourse but his trust in his Lord:

> Likewise, the governing authority should, on its own initiative or through the instigation of others, help and protect him too, without any complaint, application, or instigation on his own part. If it fails to do this, he should permit himself to be despoiled and slandered; he should not resist evil, as Christ's words say.[21]

The prevailing concern is the purity and peculiarity of the Christian's and, with him, the church's witness to the world. Christians do not look or act like every other citizen of a modern democracy.

Clearly, the implementation of these ideas is not without challenges

---

19. *LW* 45, 101.
20. Ibid.
21. Ibid.

and differences of opinion regarding the best way forward in a given situation. While violent self-defense is never warranted for the sake of self, it could possibly be justified for the sake of the self's vocational responsibilities toward dependents. And while an evening spoiled by a botched order at a restaurant should not result in a Christian demanding or even expecting appropriate restitution for her personal inconvenience, it could conceivably mean calling attention to the failure for the sake of the restaurant's success and potential future prosperity. Still, while it must be granted that there is an abundance of complicated issues open for discussion and debate, the guiding principle is not difficult to grasp, it is simply unfamiliar and difficult: Christians both as individuals and as the church do not seek their own welfare, much less ever assert or demand their own "rights."

Living without an expectation of privilege or a claim to even basic rights should also prompt an incisive and unflinching reevaluation of the church's attempts to participate in political dialogue and efforts to shape public policy and law. That the church can rightly involve itself in the world of politics has been consistently and hopefully persuasively argued and defended through the pages of this book. But an endorsement of political pursuits is certainly not a sweeping approval of any and all advocacy or activity undertaken by the church. In the context of the current discussion about the Christian refusal to think in terms of rights, it should be evident that the church must not lobby for its own benefit or seek to protect or expand whatever rights, that is to say, privileges, that the state chooses to grant. Of course, Christians are obligated to worship, evangelize, and declare God's truth into the world, but they have no inherent or even God-given right to do any of these things. Should the state remove the privileges or protections safe-guarding such activities, the church must simply disobey and endure the state's attempts to impose consequences—just as it has routinely done throughout history.

An intentional and deliberate presence in the nation's Capitol to influence and educate legislators and leaders for the sake of God's creatures who suffer injustice certainly may be an appropriate action of the church. Such advocacy, however, should never be conducted for its own sake, not even when the church itself is the victim of injustice. What Luther declares with regard to the Christian applies also to the church:

> In what concerns you and yours, you govern yourself by the gospel and suffer injustice toward yourself as a true Christian; in what concerns the person or property of others, you govern yourself according to love and tolerate no injustice toward your neighbor.[22]

The church should never champion or lobby for the preservation of its own "first amendment rights." To do so would ultimately diminish the church's identity, trivialize its proclamation, and reduce it to the level of every other self-focused human institution. In the face of the erosion of privilege and the restriction or removal of "rights," fear of dire repercussions for the church or her people must not prevail and be allowed to shape the church's course of action. The consequent penalties and persecution that could be imposed on the church that refuses to compromise its confession and practice may appear to be devastating and insurmountable. But as history amply attests, God's provision for his church always overwhelmingly surpasses all human and demonic effort to quash and crush it—no matter how punitive or violent. And it is wise to remember that regardless of their level of sanctification, humans have rarely proven to be accurate predictors of what will be beneficial or detrimental for the church. Grounded in the reality of God's truth, and therefore immune to any challenge and all debate, is the enduring fact that the church that is dismissive of herself and her own rights, yet submissive to her Lord and humble in her service will always endure and, by God's grace and according to his will, thrive.

Being Christian in America

It is the absence of what might be called individual rights, coupled with the obligations inherent in being part of God's creation that provide

---

22. *LW* 45, 96.

the necessary context for understanding Luther's strident rejection of rebellion in any form. Exhorting his readers in 1522 not to succumb to the spirit of the times and rise up in armed rebellion against the pope along with the state and the princes that supported papal hegemony, Luther expressed his contempt for insurrection and rebellion in typical fashion:

> Third, God has forbidden insurrection, where he speaks through Moses, "Quod iustum est, iuste, exequaris; Thou shalt follow justly after that which is just," and again, "revenge is mine; I will repay." Hence we have the true proverb, "He who strikes back is in the wrong," and again, "No one can be his own judge." Now insurrection is nothing else than being one's own judge and avenger, and that is something God cannot tolerate. Therefore, insurrection cannot help but make matters much worse, because it is contrary to God; God is not on the side of insurrection.[23]

The position is neither complicated, nor vulnerable to nuance or exception. Not that many valiant intellectual and theological sorties to excuse and endorse rebellion have not been mounted, of course. Christian Americans committed to their legends of the godliness and blessedness of their nation and especially its glorious, Christian, origins are particularly obliged to such undertakings. But Luther would have none of it. Authority put in place by God must be obeyed, and may be disobeyed only when its commands are in direct opposition to God's clear law. Distasteful and difficult as it may be, unjust treatment by a government is not cause for rebellion. Since there is no God-given right to hold personal property or to enjoy individual liberty, these illusory ideals cannot be invoked as just cause for armed rebellion. Christians do not take up arms against their government—not ever. This does not mean, however, that the truth lies in the diametrically opposed posture. Quietism is a sin as great as rebellion. A sin of omission damns no less than a sin of commission. Christians do not rebel, but neither do they compliantly bow to the injustice and evil of a wicked ruler or an ignorantly wrong institution. Luther, of course, understood this perfectly: "For the governing authority must not be resisted by force,

---

23. "A Sincere Admonition by Martin Luther to All Christians to Guard against Insurrection and Rebellion," *LW* 45, 63.

but only by confession of the truth."[24] Confession of the truth, the bold declaration of God's will, is the requirement binding on every follower of Christ. Christians do not take up the sword, they do not resist by force, but they do absolutely resist. What is evil must be opposed and defied even at the price of personal loss.

There is great need for a recovery of this understanding of Christian faithfulness. Many Christians seem to assume that only one of two mutually exclusive possibilities are available to guide them in their dealings with an undesirable government—whether it be maliciously unjust and immoral or merely difficult and unpleasant. One option is that exemplified by the eighteenth-century American patriots who rebelled against the British crown and, wittingly or not, God's authority, and then, wrapped their rebellion in the mantle of their purported Christian faith. This option discovers some caveat or another to skirt the scriptural injunction against rebellion, and then, foments an incendiary spirit of revolution, ready, at least in theory, once again to exercise what have become precious second amendment rights in a fight to overthrow tyranny and to preserve their sacred liberty and the nation of the founding fathers that exists, if not in their memories, then at least in their imaginations. If, however, armed resistance does not seem to fit the inclinations or perhaps convictions of the believer, then the only remaining option, it is assumed, is a studied detachment, practiced silence, and apparent indifference toward their government and its activities. The sense that a Christian must choose either between revolution, on the one hand, or quietism, on the other, is perpetuated by those in either opposing camp who interpret and characterize any challenge to their view as endorsement of the other. But this is not a problem of choosing between mutually exclusive polar opposites. Nor, it should be clear, is the solution a synthesis of the contrasting views, yielding a compromise somewhere between the extremes. The solution is to reject both rebellion and quietism, and instead, adopt the position of submissive Christian activism and resistance.

24. "Temporal Authority," *LW* 45, 124.

The specific direction that such submissive activism might take cannot be subjected to formulaic prescription. While the two extremes of armed revolt and detached quietism are both ruled out, there lies between them a vast arena in which Christians interact with the government in ways that are invariably fluid and dynamic. Each situation and each Christian will determine the best course of action at any given moment. And as always, the Christian will observe, evaluate, and act in his culture in conversation with the community of his church—both its local congregational manifestation as well as the comprehensive "una sancta" church of all times and places. The Christian's goal is clear: to speak God's truth into the world, and to act in ways that conform to God's law. The specific path toward the goal will often be far from clear, but whatever the course of action, conformity with God's law will be the *sine qua non*. Submission to God's will and God's government, coupled with active resistance against evil are not antithetical positions—though there will be times when knowing how best to maintain both will not be obvious or easy; of course, there will be other times when the right path is all too obvious, but exceedingly difficult. To denounce evil and to work to uphold God's law and justice may demand much of the faithful believer. Faithfulness may come at the price of popularity, comfort, possessions, peace, and even life itself. So be it. The Christian has no expectation of privilege or ease, and the Christian church is not unwilling to forsake temporal status, honor, property, influence, and prosperity for the sake of the proclamation of God's truth. When the world is least willing to hear that truth is precisely when the church and her people must speak it most plainly.

So, what might this look like in action? A freshman congressman elected as a political outsider with a Christian moral foundation comes to terms with the reality of political negotiations and the art of compromise, and so, supports a bill that will further restrict late term abortions, but also contains language affirming a woman's right to an abortion. A different Christian man convinced of his responsibility and ability to defend his countrymen against enemy threats, joins the military and sees active combat in the infantry fighting groups who plot and practice acts of terror against civilians. In another context, another man determines that the war being waged by his country falls short of the standards of a just war, and though he is aware that his claim may not be recognized by the state or honored by others, and that he may even be jailed for his stand, nevertheless declares himself a conscientious objector and refuses to take up arms. Though his government has labeled such behavior "hate speech," punishable by fines and imprisonment, a pastor speaks God's truth from the pulpit and declares the immorality of same-sex unions. Another pastor on the other side of the world urges his flock to join the flood of other believers and citizens overwhelming the streets of his nation's capital in a successful effort to resist the rule and force the resignation of a corrupt and unjust tyrant guilty of systematic racism, torture, and homicide. A congregation establishes a food bank and without inquiring about legal status or lifestyle, regularly provides staples to homeless and impoverished individuals and families in their community. Disparate as they are, every one of these actions are alike in springing from the fertile dynamic of the teaching of the two realms. A clear and conscious application of Luther's paradigm of the temporal and spiritual realms of God's rule underlies each of these illustrations. There is nothing canned, contrived, constraining, inherently conservative, or automatically liberal about the art and practice of living out the two realms teaching, and it is applicable at all times in every context. This is the great strength and gift of this teaching. One may not be able to predict or anticipate where a faithful practice of the paradigm will lead, but there should never be any question or doubt about the paradigm's universal relevance and dependable readiness to provide clear, and sometimes surprising, guidance in every situation.

A Hope for True Christians

Living out the reality of the teaching of the two realms has the potential for some interesting, unsettling, and often demanding courses of action. It also has the potential to be quite mundane and pedestrian, with little flash or flair—but such tame paths never fail to impose their own peculiar demands. All depends on the situation into which each Christian and each local church have been called to serve. The call of Christ to faithful service for the sake of the world is the primary thing. Such faithful service may well put one at odds with the dominant zeitgeist of the surrounding culture. Such faithful service, such faithful following of Christ, may well come at a price. Resistance and rejection should surprise no one who follows—it was promised by our Lord and has been the reality for generations of faithful believers over the course of two millennia. Still, for those accustomed to the conventional and comfortable life of the Constantinian rapprochement, the idea of a price to be paid for faithfulness can be more than a little disconcerting. Whether or not the North American church and her people are ready to admit it, we are unquestionably in a season when what is expected of a "good American" cannot be reconciled with what is expected of a faithful follower of Christ. To be a good Christian inevitably makes one a bad American.

Thus, the challenge of living wisely and earnestly in the two realms is consistently compelling and critically important. The world today desperately needs Christians willing to shoulder the challenge. Five centuries ago, in a world that was, at least nominally, comprehensively Christian, Luther famously complained that the whole world was evil and that "among thousands there is scarcely a single true Christian."[25] Perhaps he was overly pessimistic, and perhaps were he living today, for the sake of accuracy, he would revise his estimate downward. Whatever the true percentage might be, true Christians need to learn what it means to live fully in both realms of God's reign, and then they must do it. When believers live like that, even granting Luther's estimate of Christians numbering less than 1/10 of 1 percent of the population, such true Christians could not fail to make a remarkable, eternal impact on their world . . . on God's world.

---

25. *LW* 45, 91. "Temporal Authority."

6

An Essay Grounded in the Two Realms: "Story Time in America"

It has become a commonplace within Christian conversation that the Church in North America is facing increasingly stiff competition not only from other religions, but from worldviews or narratives that profess to be irreligious.[1] Those committed to the project of apologetics are likely to concur and respond by mounting spirited campaigns to counter the threat. Others, like the present writer, affirm the ultimate supremacy of the Christian account of reality and see dubious outcomes when the attackers are engaged on their own turf. When all is said and done, Christianity has no competition. Nevertheless, simply from the standpoint of undertaking the Church's mission with some degree of deliberation and effectiveness, there is value in surveying the contemporary narrative landscape and exploring the sort of life stories

---

1. An earlier version of this chapter was first presented at the September, 2013 Symposium of Concordia Seminary, St. Louis, and then published as "Story Time in America," *Pro Ecclesia* 26, no. 1 (Winter, 2016), pages unknown. It appears here with thanks to the editors of the journal as an example of one way that faithful appropriation of the two realms paradigm may manifest itself.

or worldviews or narratives that describe and drive people in North America.

To describe or even just to think about the narratives that are at work in the surrounding culture and to accomplish such a task in the space of a single chapter is more than an ambitious undertaking—it is, it must be admitted, the errand of a madman. Which is to say, that this chapter will not offer a general overview or assessment of the assortment of narratives at work today in the American context. Of course, it would be tempting to invest some time and thought considering some of the alternative narratives at work in the wider culture. It would be easy enough to craft a chapter that recounts a quick trip around the "Western-worldviews-buffet" and offers a spicy or, more probably, a rancid sample here or there. While there certainly remains a compelling attraction to following such a route, that exercise would, it seems likely, easily and speedily devolve into self-indulgence and tend merely to nurture the simmering sense of outrage and sanctimony all too typical among more conservative Christians as they survey the godlessness, wantonness, and arrogant decadence of our contemporary Western culture. It would be wonderful to serve up a sizzling diatribe against the theological naturalism described and refuted so cogently by Cornelius Hunter.[2] And it would be gratifying to savor the penetrating arguments of Timothy Keller as he tackles some of Western culture's most cherished and most inane ideas about God and religion.[3] It would be a delight to share a healthy portion of N. T. Wright's soaring refutation of those—Christian and non-Christian alike—who pine for an other-worldly, immaterial, pie-in-the-sky-in-the-sweet-bye-and-bye, version of heaven.[4] Obviously, though, this work has already been done, and it just may be that there are better things to consider in grappling with the reality of our current twenty-first-century Western context. To add to the critique does little to

2. Cornelius Hunter, *Science's Blind Spot: The Unseen Religion of Scientific Naturalism* (Grand Rapids, MI: Brazos Press, 2007).
3. Timothy Keller, *The Reason for God: Belief in an Age of Skepticism* (New York: Riverhead Books, 2008).
4. N. T. Wright, *Simply Christian: Why Christianity Makes Sense* (New York: Harper One, 2006), 217–37.

further our understanding of the culture around, and begins to seem a bit like piling-on.

It is always a bit hazardous to identify some overall spirit or mood for an entire age or culture. But for the purpose of understanding the world around us today, this is a risk worth taking and is an exercise that has the potential to yield more fruit than merely sampling from the buffet of ideas that are out there. James Edwards' book *The Plain Sense of Things* provides a sweeping and comprehensive account of the way that the Western world has conceived of religion and its place in the wider culture. He also provides the term *mood*, and its definition: "Properly understood, a mood is not fundamentally 'mental' at all. A mood is a way one comports oneself to what one finds; it is a way in which one *takes*—in which one 'sounds out' in one's actions and reactions—what there is."[5] Edwards suggests four overarching moods that have been present in the West, beginning with the "age of the gods." In this first stage that corresponds with the beginning of written history, one is profoundly aware of the mystery of the divine and seeks ways individually and communally to understand, and more importantly, assuage the gods that must be there. Whether it be the God of Exodus and Sinai or the pantheon of Olympus, "Divine might makes divine right;" avers Edwards, "salvation comes only through sacrificial submission of human autonomy to the god's will."[6] Not surprisingly, Edwards represents this mood with the figure of Moses.

With the great philosophers of Greece's golden age, the epoch of the gods gives way to the season of the forms. When this mood takes hold in the culture, it is no longer cowering subservience and submission to the arbitrary will of the god that is demanded—Manasseh and his people collectively groveling at the feet of the detestable Moloch serve as a fit example—now, it is knowledge of what is perfect that becomes the standard. Edwards detects a "movement from a cosmos governed by various and conflicting divine powers into the idea that the gods too must answer to something 'higher,' something impersonal, eternal,

5. James C. Edwards, *The Plain Sense of Things: The Fate of Religion in an Age of Normal Nihilism* (University Park, PA: Pennsylvania State University Press, 1997), 13.
6. Ibid., 18–19.

and perfect: justice itself."[7] In this second age, there is no longer a personified source and norm of all that is; this place has been supplanted by rational and perfect forms: "an a priori cosmic order that confers intelligible substance on things."[8] In the age of the forms, the sacred is the ideal. As Edwards tells the story, this age lasted well into the seventeenth century, bolstered when medieval Christian thinkers warped the Christian confession to the tenets of idealism: "Platonism for the people," as Nietzsche termed it. With God as the foundation and the guide, all reality fit neatly into "the great chain of Being."[9] Such was the age of Plato.

And then, there was Descartes. Unable to accept uncritically the foundation and the form that he had been given, Descartes's search for a solid bottom led him within to the only thing he decided he could know for sure: his own skepticism. He knew that he did not know. But that was enough. Armed with a new epistemology, he put the world back together again as it had been before, with one vital difference: the certain thing that grounded everything was no longer God; now, it was the self. Appropriately, Edwards dubs this the era of ego-subjectivity. Cartesianism and its ego-subjectivity is not especially friendly to religion. Once the culture allows itself the latitude to question the certainty of its foundation, then that foundation can no longer serve a grounding and norming role for that culture. As Edwards puts it: "If the sacredness of X can sensibly be questioned, then X is no longer sacred."[10] Indeed, the religious practices of the age of ego-subjectivity are intellectual as one strives to determine what one can know and what one can trust. Descartes, as well as his expansive progeny, is seeking, Edwards observes, "that ground of pure Being—that source of the determinable identity of things—capable of underwriting his own particular theoretical and practical

7. Ibid., 19.
8. Ibid., 20.
9. Ibid., 24.
10. Ibid., 30.

commitments."[11] Of course, this is readily recognized as the age of modernity.

While much of the world continues to busy itself with its Cartesian quest, or at least, contents itself with its Cartesian account of reality, the age of ego-subjectivity is not the end of the story. The mood of the age, Edwards contends, has left the Cartesian quest behind—mortally slain by its own weapon. In its relentless quest for truth and its demand for what is certain, with a slow and unflinching realization, the culture has been forced to admit that *every* truth can never be anything more than an assertion, or a value. Edwards explains that a value is "various social practices for constructing and enforcing stable and public agreements about 'the facts,' agreements that always and only serve some particular instance of will to power."[12] Nietzsche, it turns out, was right, and so, the Western world finds itself immersed in the cultural mood that Edwards calls "the age of transvalued values."[13] In other words, there is nothing at the bottom about which a person can be certain. There is nothing but the "self-achieved self-possession and joyful power of the Overman."[14] But he, mercifully—or regrettably, depending on one's perspective—is still yet to come.

So, where does this lead? What does all of this teach about the surrounding world in these infant years of the new millennium? The whole point of Edwards's long and thorough story of Western religiosity is to provide just this answer. Western culture, he declares, is a world dominated by the mood of normal nihilism. This is not to say that the average American, much less the average mid-Westerner, is living a brutally harsh life verging on despair in its vapid meaninglessness. Neither does it mean that people are consciously aware of their need to assert meaning, and so, deliberately strike out into new arenas of self-discovery and self-fulfillment. This is simply to say that in a world which has determined that a long and careful search for truth will yield nothing but air and foam beneath the searcher's

11. Ibid., 31.
12. Ibid., 42.
13. Ibid., 43.
14. Ibid., 45.

feet, the only thing left to do is simply to claim a reality and live it. In other words, whether aware of it or not, everyone is a nihilist and this has become the normal condition.

"As normal nihilists," Edwards writes, "we are aware of both the existence of radically alternative structures of interpretation and the fact that we ourselves lack any knockdown, noncircular way to demonstrate the self-sufficiency, solidity, or originality of our own."[15] No single story can claim a foundation that can be proven unequivocally to be true. No story. Not the story of the environmentalist. Not the story of the Trekkie. Not the story of the Packers fan. Not the story of the evolutionist. Not the story of the man who believes in the inherent goodness of man and the bond that holds us all together. Not the story of the spiritual seeker who affirms all honest yearnings for things above and encourages the individual journeys that mark the lives of people deemed spiritual. Not even the story of the theist who is certain of God and his truth and his ways. By the standards of modernity, no story is authoritatively normative. No story can claim the mantle of unshakeable and unassailable reality. All are subject to individual interpretation. All reduce to mere value.

At the heart of the age of what Edwards calls transvalued values is nothing more than the individual will to choose. "To be a normal nihilist," summarizes Edwards, "is just to acknowledge that, however fervent and essential one's commitment to a particular set of values, that's all one ever has: a commitment to some particular set of values."[16] Edwards offers the shopping mall as a telling illustration of the world of transvalued values. As easily as a savvy shopper buys a pair of deck shoes from the Dockers store, or the latest iteration of an iSomething from the Apple store, so any one can pick any value or combination of values that seem somewhat compelling—and then, dump them and start fresh whenever desired. "There are still devout Jews and Muslims and Christians around, of course," Edwards observes, "but to us they begin to look like the folks who need to wear nothing

15. Ibid., 46.
16. Ibid., 47.

184

but Polo head to foot, or those who spend all their free time arguing the advantages of IBMs over Macs. The Christian bookstore is for us just another stop in the mall."[17]

Edwards does not necessarily lament the turn to normal nihilism—considering it at least a safe place, compared to the dangers of ardent fideism, whether of a nationalistic or a religious stripe. But while he contends that there are worse things than the mall, he speculates or hopes that "there also may be things that are somewhat better."[18] The problem—a problem Edwards himself recognizes—is that even the most cursory consideration of the reality of normal nihilism confronts the honest observer with the unsettling issue of meaning. To put it bluntly: there isn't any. Self-chosen meaning, it should be apparent, is not actually meaningful. If my life, and its purposes, is founded on nothing more than a choice that I have made, then how can it actually matter or lift me through the inevitable problems of life? How can it answer the nagging questions of existence, such as "Why am I here? Why do I die? And what's the point of any of this, anyway?" Normal nihilism provides a banal existence void of the need for any unwanted strife or conflict, but void also of meaning.

In the age of normal nihilism, there is nothing that is worth dying for. Nothing. A man who forfeits his life to push a young child out of the path of a careening car has done something noble only if the value that has been chosen declares the action good. He is a hero only to those who value altruism and youth. But he could as easily be deemed an insane fool—he is, after all, prematurely dead. Regardless of the cause or the circumstance, dead is dead. Clearly, this casts an entirely new light on an array of cherished values, including, for example, patriotic sacrifice. What is a country or a people but a social construct bereft of any meaning beyond that imposed by the observer? The only available meaning is one that has been imposed. It has no base, no ground in truth. It can only pretend to be substantial. It is only a value. It is only as solid as the conviction and commitment of the one who holds it.

---

17. Ibid., 51.
18. Ibid., 56.

Of course, none of this sounds particularly new and can hardly be claimed as a malaise unique to our age. Shakespeare knew the score, and through the titular character of his Scottish play, scorned this life as "a tale told by an idiot, full of sound and fury, signifying nothing."[19] Even further back, we hear the echoes of Quoleth morosely, or is it sarcastically or sagely, decrying life as "vanity of vanities," or as another translation has it, "meaningless, meaningless."[20] Yet, there is a critical and fatal difference today. Today, there is no hope. There is no enlightened individual who can grope his way back into the dark of the cave, twist stiff, uncooperative heads to look at the light, and coax a few to the truth of enlightenment. Today, the enlightened individual knows that there is no light besides the torch or headlamp that I choose. Today, the light to which one crawls is as likely the light of a hurtling locomotive. In the present age, there is no hope. There is no possibility of experiencing a warm glow that fills the breast and stretches tingling like electricity into the extremities when life is suddenly caught up in the glory of the divine. Religious conversion, it is now known, is nothing more than the vain dreams and desperate delusions of those who would seek solace and wrest meaning out of an empty universe. Regardless of how it feels, or inspires, or makes sense, or fires the creative imagination, faith in God—any God—is, as every honest and thinking normal nihilist knows, nothing more than another choice—a value.

Normal nihilism is the story, the only story, which is at work in the world around us. Stanley Hauerwas concurs with Edwards's penetrating assessment, and with his peculiar penchant for turning a phrase, offers this way of understanding the current situation: "the project of modernity was to produce people who believe they should have no story except the story they choose when they have no story."[21] The remarkable and somewhat startling outcome of this evaluation of contemporary Western culture, then, is that it really does not make

---

19. William Shakespeare, *Macbeth*, Act V, Scene V.
20. Ecclesiastes 1:2 (NASB, NIV).
21. Stanley Hauerwas, *Sanctify Them in the Truth: Holiness Exemplified* (Nashville, TN: Abingdon, 1998), 197–98.

any difference what stories people are telling and believing in the world around us. None of them matter. Every single last one is nothing but a value, nothing but a choice. It has no substance. Consequently, the need for the church to argue against, and so, expose and dismantle false stories has essentially evaporated. The pitiless, relentless, and mind-numbingly boring glare of normal nihilism's indiscriminate sun burns hot on every person and every idea and withers away the life of both story and person. Nothing is left but a husk; and one husk is as good as another. Human life is reduced to making choices between competing husks, that is, values—an enterprise that resembles shopping at the mall less than it does hermit crabs on the beach scrounging for a better shell. The church does not need to worry overmuch then, about what people are believing these days. In reality, people are not believing much of anything.

What is the church supposed to do? Once again, Hauerwas has some suggestions that are worth hearing. For starters, the church must not succumb to old temptations and tired notions of seeking relevance and importance for itself in the push and shove world of the shopping mall. No one ever really liked shopping at Zondervan anyway, and who will really be sorry to see the end of mass-produced plaques of the "Footprints" poem and predictable and poorly written books about the scriptural path to successful marriage, parenting, sexual contentment, and retirement—roughly in that order. Christians must repent of trying to sell the church by trying to make her attractive to the wider culture. The church is the bride of Christ, not a whore to be fit to the whims of the clientele culture. "Christians in modernity," observes Hauerwas, "thought their task was to make the Gospel intelligible to the world rather than to help the world understand why it could not be intelligible without the Gospel."[22] In other words, the task of the church is not to find its way into the world—mankind's culture built on the folly and in the fallout of the first sin—and establish a beachhead there. The task is boldly and stubbornly to insist to the world that the only possible way the world and its inhabitants can ever matter is for

22. Ibid., 193.

the world to see itself within the story of the church—the concrete reality of Christ at work among and through his elect people.

The world does not like this. Still, it should be clear, both from the weight of this argument and from personal experience, that the world does *not* entirely begrudge people of faith their chosen value. In fact, the world is, at times, almost giddy with curiosity about what makes people of faith tick. Some years ago when a deranged man lined up young girls in an Amish schoolroom and shot them in turn, the world was understandably fixated on the event. It was not only the stark horror, though, that held their gaze. It was the oddity of the people involved and the absurdity of their response. These idiosyncratic people breathed words not of anger and hate, but of meekness and forgiveness. The world was mesmerized. Reporters spoke with awe and appreciation for the wonder of these strange Americans who were so unlike the rest of us. The faith of the Amish was wonderful when it was being held and practiced by the Amish. Similarly, for any other group who lives with profound convictions of faith. Normal nihilism applauds such lifestyles: live and let live, each can choose the values he likes. David Yeago gets it exactly right:

> That human beings make their inward apprehension of meaning available to others in poetic and symbolic form; that those who share similar spiritual aspirations band together in voluntary associations for mutual support; that the inner light of religious experience motivates the way in which individuals and groups make choices amongst public options—these have been widely accepted and welcomed in all but the crudest anti-religious fringes of the dominant culture of the past two centuries.[23]

As long as those people of faith are minding their own business and allowing others to mind theirs, then all is well. Live and let live. "It is quite different, however," Yeago continues, "when religious people make claims that involve God's immediate presence in some concrete shaping or ordering of the public world."[24] A church with the audacity to suggest a particular form of life that is normative for all people, or

---

23. David Yeago, "Sacramental Lutheranism as the End of the Modern Age," *Forum* (Winter, 2000): 6.
24. Ibid.

to question the truthfulness of a false story, or to offer healing to those suffering from the wounds of false stories, is something altogether unacceptable. Such actions defy the tenets of normal nihilism. Yeago understands this well:

> Then a whole vocabulary of denigration is brought immediately to bear, and a whole strategy of repression comes into play. Such claims are superstition, fundamentalism; they violate the boundaries of religion and science or religion and public life; they will bring back the wars of religion.[25]

God forbid.

Indeed, confronted with the prospect of a long, ugly, bloody war with the culture, Christians know what to do. The reasonable, compassionate, and above-all-else loving thing to do is, of course, to surrender. But certainly, no one calls it that. There are delicate and intelligent euphemisms for something as repugnant as surrender. The church progresses, it accommodates, Christians reach out, they adapt and adopt, and the church contextualizes and modernizes. It is true that the church's proclamation and the church's life must be translated so that the world around can hear and apprehend it, but it is crucial that Christians recognize and *practice* the acute difference between translation and capitulation. Providing the scripture in the vernacular of the people is translation. Proposing that perhaps there are others avenues of salvation besides Christ alone is capitulation. Embracing stringed instrumentation in the divine service is translation. Rewriting the understanding of fellowship and unity at the communion rail to account for a culture that has chosen the value of diversity is capitulation. Scheduled campus dialogues between scholars who hold an orthodox Christian confession and those who insist on an atheistic materialist account of reality is translation. Renovating Christian chapels into generic "spiritual centers" is capitulation. These examples of capitulation should be obvious enough, though it seems likely that even in corners of the church claiming faithfulness, they are less

---

25. Ibid.

apparent than it might be hoped. Examples of accommodation and surrender could easily be multiplied. The problem is not that the church has failed to figure out how to confront the normal nihilism that surrounds it on all sides. The problem—indeed, the crisis for the church—is that the normal nihilism that names and norms our culture is not just "out there." It is firmly entrenched in our own pews and in our own pulpits.

The church is the bride of Christ, Christ's very body at work in this world proclaiming his truth, living out his story. The church knows the reality of God's story. The church knows, as Hauerwas puts it, that "Israel and the church are not characters in a larger story called 'world,' but rather 'world' is a character in God's story as known through the story that is the church."[26] To say it another way, the world goes on inside the story of the church and not the other way around. The church knows these things—at least, it should know these things. But the nihilism that grips the culture also grips the church's pastors. It is worth hearing Hauerwas at length on this point:

> The ministry seems captured in our time by people who are desperately afraid they might actually be caught with a conviction at some point in their ministry that might curtail future ambition. They, therefore, see their task to "manage" their congregations by specializing in the politics of agreement by always being agreeable. The preaching such a ministry produces is designed to reinforce our presumed agreements, since a "good church" is one without conflict. You cannot preach about abortion, suicide, or war because those are such controversial subjects—better to concentrate on "insights" since they do so little work for the actual shaping of our lives and occasion no conflict.[27]

The impact of normal nihilism on the thinking and the conduct of the church's pastors extends beyond what is or is not said in the pulpit. It reaches to the very definition of what it means to be church. When the church, along with her ministers, is confused about her own identity, the story that defines and guides her will be equally confused . . . or absent altogether.

26. Hauerwas, *Sanctify Them in the Truth*, 192.
27. Ibid., 195.

The Christian story puts the church at odds with the world around. Of course, it should always be borne in mind that the Christian story is, in fact, God's story—one that begins before the first word of creation and continues through the eschatological consummation into eternity. To live the Christian story is simply to hear God's call and to receive all that he gives through his living Word, delivered in the means entrusted to his church. Concurrently, to live the Christian story is to endure the continual barrage of attacks stemming ultimately from Satan and serving God's plan (his story for us) by driving us at last further into the enduring grace of Christ, our only hope in the face of what Luther termed our *anfechtung*. Conflict between God's story and the world's false stories is inevitable. It cannot be otherwise. The story that the church has been given to tell does not accommodate itself to the wider culture. The church cannot abridge and censor her own story to mollify the sensitivities of normal nihilists. The church does not tolerate false stories. And as every Western citizen knows, a lack of tolerance is, in our world, the unpardonable sin. To embrace and to live the Christian story of God's election, creation, redemption, resurrection, restoration, and consummation is to invite the scorn, the vitriol, and the attacks of the world. It is to be at war.

The church's pastors should be leading the church's people to know and to live the story of Christ. Sadly, though, "In the name of love and peace," Hauerwas insists, "Christian preaching has reinforced the 'normal nihilism' that grips our lives."[28] Christians do not recognize the reality of warring stories already engaged, and they refuse to acknowledge the wars that need to be engaged because it seems "irrational that some should kill others in the name of 'values.'"[29] Indeed, to die or to kill for what is only a value is patently absurd, and in the world of normal nihilism, values and interpretation of reality is all that there is—even within the church. Perhaps this is a significant factor in the nonchalance that so often attends Christian people when they come to the divine service and to the Lord's Table. And perhaps

28. Ibid., 196.
29. Ibid.

normal nihilism in the pews offers some explanation for the relative ease with which people enter and leave churches as they shop for the one that best meets their needs—or, more accurately, coheres with the values that they choose.

The non-story of normal nihilism, that is the anti-story that eviscerates every story, is an unavoidable reality that brooks no rival. None can withstand its power to flatten and deflate every story. Such is the crushing and demoralizing fruit of man's grand experiment of Enlightenment. And there is no going back. The world can only plod ahead in its mirthless bleak nihilism—story-less and meaningless.

So, what are those who know the church and her story to do? Certainly, they should not throw up their hands, or throw in the towel, and join the world in its ennui and futility. Neither do they insist that the only course is to go back. It is foolhardy and faithless to seek to recapture or repristinate a past age when truth still mattered or when the gods were revered. God's story does not go back. It drives forward, and so must faithful followers of Christ. What Christians must do is follow the only God who is, the only God who created all that is, including the present age teeming with normal nihilists. This God is God. He reigns and he redeems his fallen and rebellious creation. This Christians know, because he has called and claimed, made and redeemed them. This is what it means to live in the awareness of the essential contingency of creatureliness. People who follow God's story in Christ learn, as Hauerwas describes it, "that our lives are intelligible only to the extent that we discover we are characters in a narrative we did not create."[30] And this realization and admission, this confession of creaturely contingency within God's plan "produces not tolerance, but humility."[31] This is what God's story—the world's only true and real story does. "The great magic of the Gospel," writes Hauerwas, "is providing us with the skills to acknowledge our life, as created, without resentment and regret."[32] That is the story that Christians tell. That is the story that Christians live.

30. Ibid., 199.
31. Ibid.
32. Ibid., 198–99.

With humility and with urgency and with a zeal borne out of conviction, experience, and the reality of God's action in their lives, Christians must enter the fray. They engage the enemy who would have them throw down their weapons and succumb to the world's normal nihilism. The church's weapons, as even Hauerwas knows, are nothing but the tools by which God makes himself known and by which he extends his story into human lives. The weapons the church wields are Word and Sacrament. The church's people preach the story. They celebrate the story as it impacts their lives at the font and at the rail, and they live the story in their homes, in their relationships, in their goals, in their habits, in their lives. Normal nihilism is pervasive. It denigrates Christian churches. It robs the life of the church's people. The solution is not to capitulate, but to proclaim and to practice God's story. The way forward is for the church's people to work with deliberate diligence to inculcate God's story into the very fabric of the lives of those entrusted to their care—their children, their students, their parishioners, their co-workers, their neighbors. The world has no enthusiasm, indeed no tolerance for the story that the church preaches and the story that her people live. So be it. The world has no story. God's people have God's story. Whether it knows it or not, the world needs desperately to hear and to see the truth of that story. With humility, but with no shame, Christians must go and tell it to them.

Suggested Further Reading

Benne, Robert. *The Paradoxical Vision: A Public Theology for the Twenty-First Century*. Minneapolis, MN: Fortress Press, 1995.

Bonhoeffer, Dietrich. *Ethics*. "Christ, Reality and Good." Translated by Neville Horton Smith. New York: Simon & Schuster, 1955.

Cranz, F. Edward. *An Essay on the Development of Luther's Thought on Justice, Law, and Society*. Mifflinton, PA: Sigler Press, 1998.

Hunter, James Davison. *To Change the World: The Irony, Tragedy, and Possibility of Christianity in the Late Modern World*. Oxford: Oxford University Press, 2010.

Neuhaus, Richard John. *American Babylon: Notes of a Christian Exile*. Philadelphia, PA: Basic Books, 2010.

Siemon-Netto, Uwe. *The Fabricated Luther: The Rise and Fall of the Shirer Myth*. St. Louis, MO: Concordia, 1995.

Witte, John Jr. *Law and Protestantism: The Legal Teachings of the Lutheran Reformation*. Cambridge: Cambridge University Press, 2002.

Index